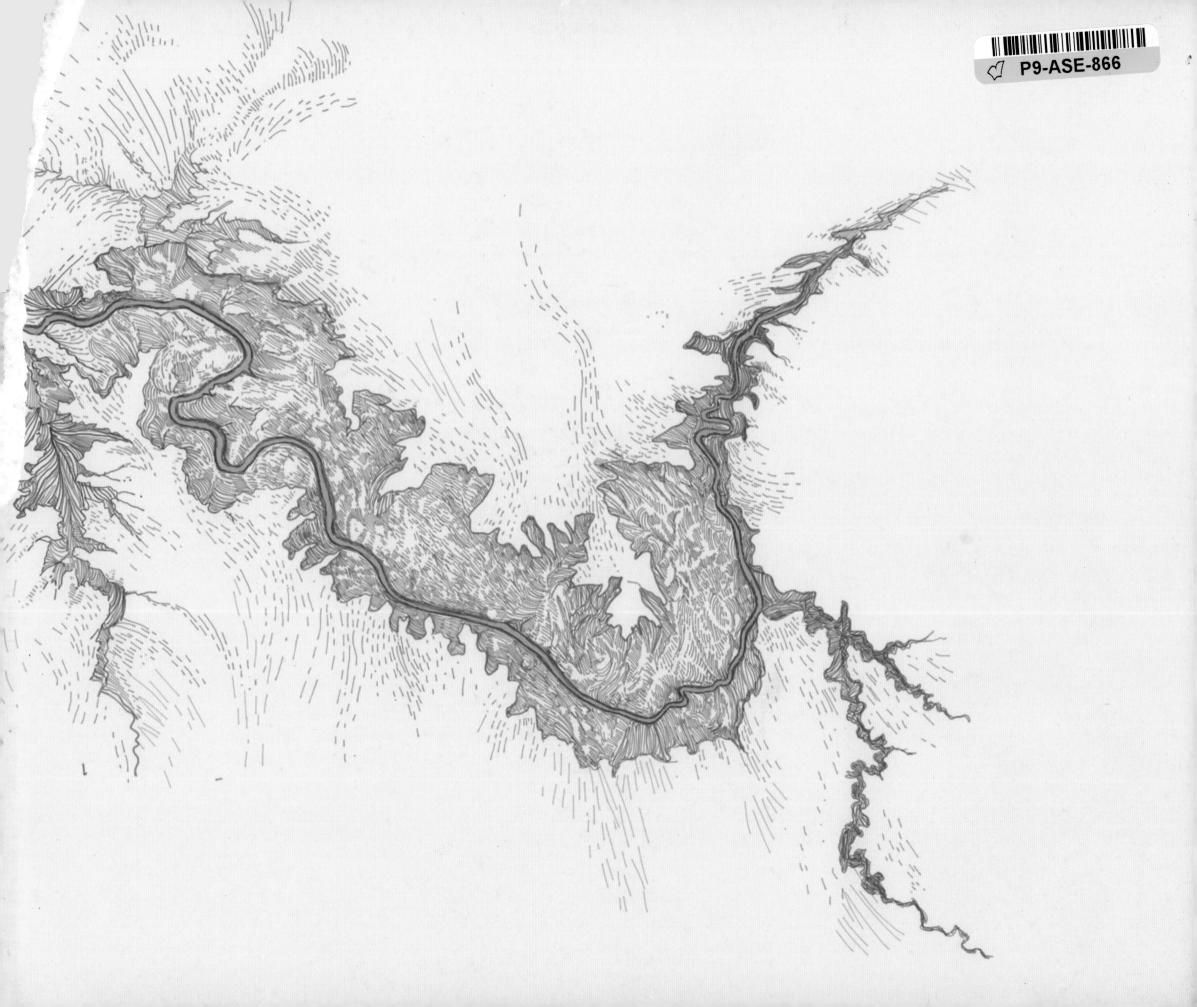

THE GRAND CANYON

THE GRAND CANYON

BETWEEN RIVER AND RIM

PETE McBRIDE

Foreword by HAMPTON SIDES

Introduction by KEVIN FEDARKO

Grand Canyon Association

RIZZOLI
NEW YORK

New York Paris London Milan

TO MY PARENTS   MOUTIE AND PABO   THANKS FOR TEACHING ME THE POWER OF PLACE

CONTENTS

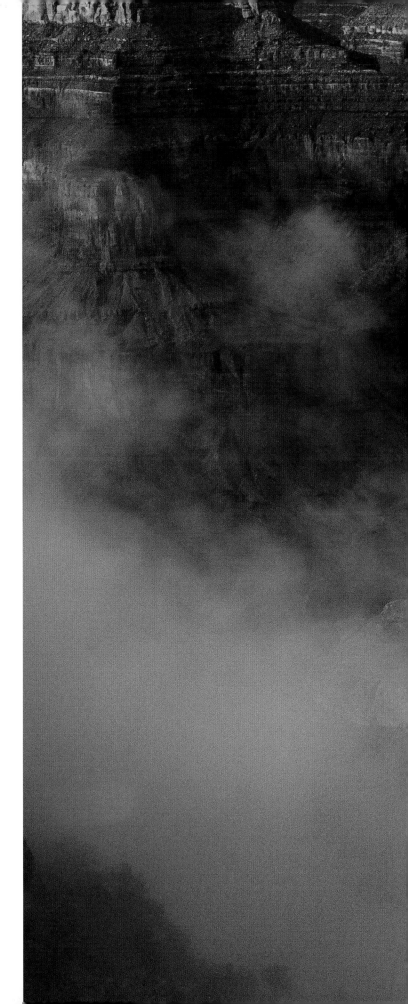

FOREWORD

HAMPTON SIDES

Let's not hide our light under a bushel: the Grand Canyon of Arizona is our mightiest of landscapes. It is the Big Ditch, the Mother Groove, the Timeless Fold. And the river that carved it is the Ganges of the American environmental movement, the hallowed waterway of John Wesley Powell, David Brower, and Edward Abbey. Mile for mile, it's perhaps the most regulated, most studied, and most politicized gulch on the planet. There is simply nothing like it.

Sadly, most people only see it from up high, from a crowded "scenic lookout." They peer down into the abyss, dutifully awestruck and mystified. Then they hop back in their cars. It's grand all right, but there's just too much there there: too much to take in, too much to see and think about, too much to *feel*.

And to be honest, there's something a little scary about it. It's a terrain stamped with terrific violence, on a scale that dwarfs human beings, not only spatially but also chronologically. It suggests chasms of time that mock our relevance in the story of creation.

To even begin to understand the Grand Canyon, you have to put in some sweat equity. You have to get down in there and fuss with those puzzles of water and rock. You have to explore the broiled mazes, the slot canyons, the endless notches and alcoves. You have to read the runes. This takes a lot of effort, more effort than most people are willing or able to expend. Most people are content to let the thereness be.

I'm certainly no expert on the Grand Canyon, but I've experienced it a half-dozen times, on foot and by boat. I've walked across it, rim to rim. I've felt its seductions. I get why Barry Goldwater once said that if he were to have one, this place would be his mistress. I get why another

Mist rolls past the layers of rock and time inside the central corridor.

Arizona politician, John McCain, has said that although he subscribes to evolution, he also believes, when he hikes the Grand Canyon, "the hand of God is there." Something about the place curiously inclines one's thoughts toward the scientific, and yet simultaneously, toward the theological, which may be a pretty good definition for "magic."

Walking over it, rafting through it, camping in it, we feel squishably insignificant—a feeling that I find paradoxically uplifting. To me, it's a source of comfort to know that we're nothing, that nature always wins, and that, in the end, we *Homo not-so-sapiens* are mere spore specks in the record of time. When you get down in there, and drift deep in those ancient curves of rock, there is something the guides like to call "river time." It's the sense that the clock is standing still, and that the vexations of the "real" world have ceased to matter. With it comes the paradoxical counterawareness that our own time here on earth is mighty short, and we'd better spend every precious minute of it doing things that make us happy—surrounding ourselves with good companions, pursuing meaningful work, losing ourselves in the immensity of great places.

I was introduced to the canyon a couple dozen years ago by a wise, dry-witted guy named Dugald Bremner. I found myself riding down the Colorado with Dugald in his beloved dory, the *Skagit*. It was a historic time to be out on the river; the Bureau of Reclamation that very week had released massive amounts of water from the penstocks of Glen Canyon Dam in a controversial experiment to mimic the ancient spring snowmelt floods—and thus to blow out the accumulated silt from the river channel. For those of us downstream, this epic federal experiment meant something else: record high water, and exhilarating, sometimes terrifying, hydraulics.

Dugald was well known in the rarefied world of the hard-core canyon rats. Born in Scotland, he had longish hair, a sun-leathered face, and a Celtic twinkle in his sharp hazel eyes. He was a purist of the canyon experience, and he treated his dory like a beautiful woman. "She's graceful in repose," he liked to say in an exaggerated brogue, "but high and dry in the heavygoing." Dugald has since passed away. He died in 1997 in a kayaking accident in California, and his remains were spread—where else?—in the Grand Canyon.

To watch Dugald at the oars of the *Skagit* was like watching a gifted sprinter run or a great chef cook. It was the thing he was born to do. Whenever we approached a big hissing rapid, Dugald would sit up in his dory, calmly attuned to every swirling detail, occasionally making the tiniest corrective flick of an oar tip. If I seemed apprehensive about

The challenge of moving through Marble Canyon by foot involves finding a line through a network of stomach-turning ledges.

Hiking the length of the canyon on foot is daunting. Navigating the "jumping" cholla cactus is just one challenge (above). Throughout the journey, our bodies started to bend to the canyon's heat, contours, and rhythms (opposite).

life they'd chosen, sure of their belief that the staggering place they'd spent so much of their adult lives mastering was the closest thing we had to Xanadu.

Don't worry—I won't go overboard here. Writers hoping to capture in words that ineffable whatever-it-is about the Grand Canyon must proceed at their own risk. Most attempts at describing it tend toward the purple or the pseudocosmic. What can one say about the place that wasn't better said, long ago, by some wise and eloquent soul? It's the kind of landscape that gives the poet in all of us just enough rope to hang himself.

What is perhaps more instructive to talk about is not so much the canyon itself as the kind of people the canyon attracts—the kind of people who, like Dugald, fall madly in love with it, become enmeshed in it, become afflicted by it. Photographer Pete McBride and his hiking compadre Kevin Fedarko are two such people. As you'll see, they have the affliction something bad—which is really, really good for us. They're a perfect example of the peculiar kind of ambition the Grand Canyon inspires, a perfect example of the way it leads certain intrepid individuals in the direction of superlatives. Go big or go home, the canyon seems to tell us. The great American philosopher Evel Knievel summed it up when he said, "You can't say you're going to jump the Grand Canyon and then jump some other canyon."

So you hold in your hands a remarkable paean to one of earth's most remarkable places: not some other canyon, but the one that matters most. This sumptuous volume is a kind of testament to the irresistible pull that this magnificent landscape exerts over human beings. It tells the story of two resourceful, adventurous, and probably sadomasochistic dudes who, at some peril and much personal hardship, decided to do something very few people had ever done: walk the full length of it.

When we say "walk" it, we're not talking about some stroll down a nicely marked and immaculately maintained rim trail. We're talking about getting down into the crazy guts of the thing, down into that great no-man's-land between river and rim. Pete and Kevin went on a series of bushwhacking, boulder-hopping, scree-slipping odysseys. What they experienced was a whole lot of wonder and a whole lot of pain. It was a journey that could be measured in miles but was perhaps better captured by other metrics: numbers of blisters accumulated, of cactus stab wounds endured, of heat strokes narrowly avoided. By traversing the Grand Canyon in the hardest imaginable way, these two stalwart gentlemen managed to create (at times) a living hell for themselves, right in the middle of paradise.

a particularly gnarly passage, he would say, by way of reassurance, "Look, it's only water. It's not like there's going to be . . . *snipers*." And as we dropped effortlessly through the froth, there was no wasted motion, no yahoo theatrics, no desperate straining at the oars. Just a sure clean line through the water, and a quiet measured smile on his face.

Dugald once told me, only half-facetiously, that he was a member of the "high church of the canyon." And as I watched him there, rowing in his temple, I found myself thinking, with a mixture of envy and awe, how many of us are ever so lucky to find a faith as joyful as this? Like all the veteran river runners, he knew every coming kink and eddy and could draw in the sand the exact layout of each rapid. Hance. Sockdolager. Horn Creek. Granite. Crystal. Lava. He and his fellow canyon rats could speak of the nuances in an intimate, fraternal shorthand, sounding like a bunch of old linksmen discussing a certain enigmatic hole at Muirfield or St. Andrews. They were understated elitists, sure of their craft, sure of the proud if not especially remunerative

Why did they do it? They can explain it far better than I can—and their words and pictures in the pages ahead do just that, with much poignancy and grace. But from what I can tell, they mainly did it because they couldn't help themselves. Like I say, the Grand Canyon has an immeasurably powerful effect on certain people, and it makes them do powerfully strange and amazing things.

They did it, also, because the canyon is in big trouble. It's hard to think of something so immense and implacable as being fragile. But it is. The crown jewel of the national park system faces far more threats than most of us realize. The extent and relentless intensity of mammon's interest in the canyon, the incorrigible instinct to make dollars off this most sacred of our public grounds, cried out for a pilgrimage, big and brash and bold.

And so Pete and Kevin set out on their adventure, reconfirming the essential truth that mystics and penitents of all stripes have known for millennia: put one foot in front of the other, and brilliant things will follow.

A double rainbow graces the canyon northeast of Kanab Creek.

OVERLEAF
Looking for the route ahead on the ancient shoulders of the greatest river in the American Southwest.

I do not know, really,

how we will survive without places

like the Grand Canyon to visit.

Once in a lifetime, even, is enough.

BARRY LOPEZ, *Crossing Open Ground*

INTRODUCTION

KEVIN FEDARKO

EXACTLY 102 YEARS SINCE ITS INCEPTION IN 1916, THE US national park system now boasts a network of more than 417 parks, monuments, and other sites, all of them studded like the gemstones of an immense coronation cape whose hemline extends from the coast of Florida to the Pacific Ocean, and whose collar stretches across the neck of the Arctic Circle.

People are often surprised to learn that within those folds, the Grand Canyon actually falls a notch or two short of the number-one position according to almost every conventional metric by which supremacy is conventionally judged. It fails to qualify as either the first park in the system—a distinction that belongs to Yellowstone—or the largest (Alaska's Wrangell-St. Elias is nearly seven times bigger). It's also not the most popular park. (Great Smoky Mountains, which straddles North Carolina and Tennessee, draws almost twice as many visitors each year.)

As for the canyon itself, it's certainly not the deepest declivity on earth (which is located in Peru or Tibet, depending on how you're measuring) or the longest (which is on the Indian subcontinent) or the widest (look to Australia for that). In fact, it doesn't even contain the oldest rocks on earth, which are found in Canada.

And yet few would argue that this mile-deep abyss in northern Arizona, a vast amphitheater of sun-dappled stone that was sculpted over uncountable eons by the Colorado River, stands not only as the centerpiece of America's national park system, but also the touchstone of the nation's topography and geology. A place whose contours, instantly recognizable to virtually every citizen of this country, affirm it as "one of

The tangerine light of sunrise sweeps into Marble Canyon below Eminence Break.

the great sights," in the words of President Theodore Roosevelt, "which every American, if he can travel at all, should see."

Roosevelt's first encounter with the canyon was exceptionally brief: those words were part of a speech he gave during an eight-hour stopover at the south rim in May 1903. Despite the fleeting nature of his visit, however, the force of the canyon's magnificence, the dignity of its bearing, the austerity of its silences, and above all the gorgeous indifference with which its vast interior furnishes a sweeping backdrop for an endlessly shifting interplay of light and shadow across every hue that can register on the human eye or heart—all of that struck the president like the blow of a hammer.

Indeed, the impact was so powerful it convinced Roosevelt, the quintessential man of action, that the best thing one could possibly do with the place was to back off and leave it alone: "I hope you will not have a building of any kind, not a summer cottage, a hotel, or anything else, to mar the wonderful grandeur, the sublimity, the loneliness and beauty of the canyon," he admonished his audience, many of whom were boosters hell-bent on making a buck off the land by mining minerals, harvesting timber, grazing cattle, or fleecing tourists.

"Leave it as it is," he told them. "Man cannot improve on it; not a bit."

Whether he realized it or not, when Roosevelt uttered that statement, he was touching upon an abiding truth that has been self-evident to almost anyone who has ever stood on the canyon's rim, gazed into its depths, and understood that this, more than anything else, is the primary credo that should govern how we treat this space.

IF THE GRAND CANYON CAN BE SAID TO HAVE A SINGLE DEFINING feature, it is surely the stair-stepped walls of rock that thrust upward like immense palisades from both sides of the Colorado River. Encased within those ramparts, which claw more than a mile into the sky, is a stratified record of the past—more than 26 layers of stone whose story can be deciphered and read much like the pages of a book.

The youngest of those layers, which comprise the canyon's rim, dates back almost 250 million years to a period directly after the greatest catastrophe the world has ever known, an extinction event known as the Great Dying, in which 96 percent of all marine species and almost three-quarters of terrestrial vertebrates were wiped from the face of the earth.

By contrast, the oldest of those rock layers, the coal-black Vishnu schist that forms the subbasement of the canyon, boasts a bloodline extending back almost two *billion* years, a span of time that represents

A raven's view reveals the fractured, layered landscape of the park, famous for its daily dance of light and shadow.

one-third the age of the planet, and nearly a tenth the lifespan of the universe itself. When that rock was first formed, multicellular organisms had yet to evolve and the only things alive anywhere on earth were whorled chains of the earliest cyanobacteria, anaerobic creatures whose chemistry had coalesced shortly after the crust of the planet had begun to cool.

The sweep of stone bracketed between the top and bottom of the canyon thus represents the finest exposure of rock, over time, anywhere on the planet. And although the value of those walls is often celebrated purely in terms of aesthetics—their shape, their texture, the symphonic pageantry of color that plays across their surfaces each morning and again each evening—the true worth of all that rock and all that time transcends beauty in a way that renders visual delight all but irrelevant.

There are surely places of equal and perhaps, some might argue, even greater loveliness—places as wondrous and varied as the Redwood-pillared cathedrals of Northern California, the ice-etched escarpments of the Tetons, or the emerald-studded canopies of the Everglades. But nowhere else on earth are the forces that forged and framed the planet itself revealed with such naked, titanic candor. And by extension, nowhere else on earth do the works and aspirations of humankind seem so puny, so insignificant by comparison.

Nowhere else, anywhere, can we gaze upon something so clearly beyond ourselves and thereby be forced to acknowledge how small we truly are.

All of which makes for a rather striking irony. Because as our country's national park system passes over the threshold of its first centennial, this canyon, this monumental testament to the insignificance of mankind, may no longer be able to transmit with sufficient force its central insight, the idea that we most need to hear. A message that touches upon the thing we Americans most lack, which is humility.

From every point on the compass, from the air above as well as the ground below, the integrity of the Grand Canyon is under threat from people seeking to profit from its wonders, cutting directly against the principle that Roosevelt laid out. In so doing, these developers are poised to inflict irreparable harm on the canyon's treasures, many of which are so deeply buried within its twisted labyrinth of buttes, towers, and tributary drainages that they have been seen by almost no one.

From the east, a group of businessmen in Phoenix is partnering with members of the Navajo Nation to promote a cable-driven tramway

A long exposure reveals the headlamp trail of hikers exiting the Bright Angel Trail to the south rim, where roughly six million visitors experience the park annually. Tusayan Village glows in the distance beneath a sweep of starlight.

OVERLEAF
The confluence of the turquoise Little Colorado River and the main Colorado is believed sacred by many Native American tribes that live around the canyon. A billion-dollar tram proposal is highlighting the vulnerability of the national park's neighboring lands.

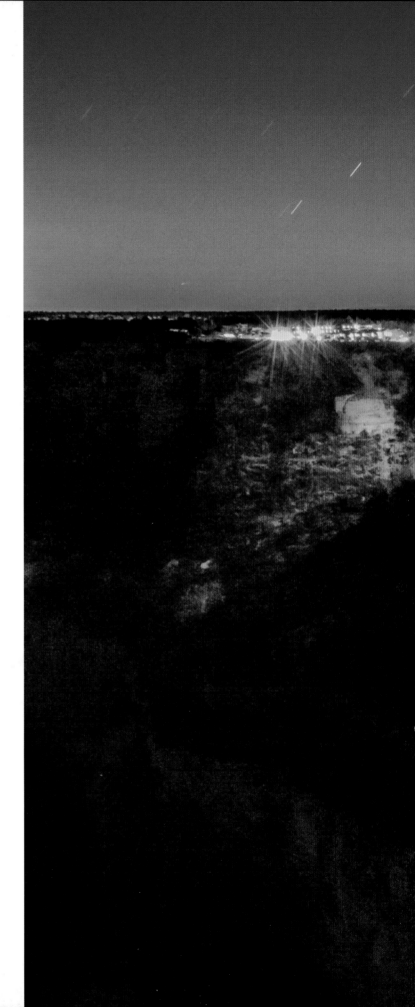

capable of delivering up to 10,000 tourists a day from the rim of the canyon to a walkway and restaurant along the river at its bottom.

Meanwhile, the north and south rims of the canyon are dotted with uranium mines, some defunct and others quite active. The shafts and tailings of those mines, along with a real-estate project that is simultaneously being planned for the south rim, threaten the aquifers that are responsible for driving many of the springs and seeps that serve as biological linchpins to the ecosystem in the heart of the canyon.

Finally, off to the west, air-tour operators based in Las Vegas are partnering with the Hualapai tribe to fill the canyon corridor with a daily stream of between 300 and 500 helicopters. These machines—whose noise can be heard from up to 20 miles away virtually without cessation from shortly after sunrise to just before sunset, seven days a week, 365 days a year—are destroying one of the canyon's most fragile and precious treasures, which is its soundscape of silence.

It's no exaggeration to say that virtually every part of this vast wilderness—what is recognized by all, what is familiar to only a few, and what yet remains a secret to everyone—is now for sale. And for this very reason, the canyon also offers up one of the most provocative locations not only to celebrate the riches that America's national park system contains, but also to take a measure of forces that are now arrayed against those very same parks.

As it turns out, however, that's a rather tall order.

Thanks to the canyon's topographic and geologic complexity, cataloguing its hidden wonders while simultaneously gauging the threats that are poised to harm those gems isn't something that can be pulled off by moving through the canyon's interior swiftly, or through conventional means.

You simply cannot conduct this kind of assessment by standing on the rim and gazing in (as nearly six million visitors do each year), or by flying over the park in a helicopter or a fixed-wing aircraft (as tens of thousands of air-tour passengers do each year). Nor can you accomplish this goal by cruising along the bottom in a boat, as another 26,000 river runners do each year.

The bulk of the canyon's interior consists of a matrix of cliffs and ledges, tributary gorges, and slot canyons that are not only inaccessible from the rims or the river, but also invisible from these vantages. To know this world, you must see it through the eyes of a foot soldier, which is to say, from the ground. And the only way to do that is to cut a transect through the heart of this landscape by lugging your gear and your provisions on your back, and by stumbling from one hidden

The hidden jewels of the canyon are the springs that most often emerge inside slot canyons. These fresh oases help sustain one of the widest ranges of biodiversity in any national park.

OVERLEAF
Dappled light dances across the eastern canyon, showcasing layers of rock that date back 1.7 billion years, roughly one-third of the earth's age.

pocket of water to the next. Day by day, week by week, month by month until you have walked from the canyon's eastern entry point at Lees Ferry to its western terminus at the Grand Wash Cliffs, a distance of 750-plus miles.

Adding to the many challenges of this approach is the inconvenient fact that there is no path one can follow. In fact, unlike the Appalachian Trail, Pacific Crest Trail, or Continental Divide Trail, when you are deep inside the Grand Canyon the word "trail" simply doesn't apply. For the most part, forging a route involves a nightmarish bushwhack across a vertical desert graced by stark ruination and savage beauty. A landscape haunted by far too little water and far too much of God's indifference to ever make it seem anything but hostile and downright mean.

And that, in a nutshell, is precisely what the photographer and filmmaker Pete McBride set out to do in the autumn of 2015.

PETE INVITED ME TO TAG ALONG WITH HIM BECAUSE WE ARE friends, and because we have had many adventures together. But my presence as a writer was never more than a kind of coda or afterthought. Which, I hasten to add, was entirely fitting, because the canyon is a place where words tend to lose their power and are forced to take a back seat to images—a fact that no one understood better than the canyon's first and greatest modern-day explorer.

"The wonders of the Grand Canyon cannot be adequately represented in symbols of speech, nor by speech itself," declared Major John Wesley Powell, the one-armed Civil War veteran who led the first river journey in recorded history through the canyon, and who stands as perhaps the only person who commands a greater stature inside this place than Roosevelt.

"The resources of the graphic art are taxed beyond their powers in attempting to portray its features," Powell wrote of the canyon. "Language and illustration combined must fail."

Well, as it turns out, the major was both right and wrong about that. It's true, words do fail, and drawings don't fare much better. But Powell's first expedition in the summer of 1869 neglected to include a photographer—and thus he had no way of fathoming that this medium comes closer than any other to capturing what the canyon *actually* looks and feels like.

In Pete's eyes, then, the purpose of his quest was twofold.

On the one hand, he saw us embarking on a venture that might provide a valedictory summary of the features inside this place that we,

as a nation, have managed to protect and preserve for future generations of Americans.

On the other hand, he would also be composing a visual requiem for those gems that are now in the process of being discarded.

And above both of those objectives hovered the same question: Are we breaking Roosevelt's covenant to leave this place intact—to "keep it for your children and your children's children and for all who come after you"?

In the end, the answer to that question cannot be captured in any sequence of words that I might string together on the page. Instead, the lessons and insights our journey bequeathed achieve their most provocative expression in the images that Pete brought home, images that are now laid before you in the pages of this book.

As you move through those pages, bear in mind that they offer up an elegy for an incomparable landscape, a place like no other, and the magic it once held in the palm of its hand. Whether that magic remains or disappears will depend, in large part, on the actions of people like you.

A juniper tree stands atop an age-tinted Esplanade shelf west of the Dome.

OVERLEAF
Embracing the warmth of a winter sunrise some 3,000 feet above the river on the western rim of Forster Canyon.

You've got to walk, better yet,

crawl, on hands and knees over the sandstone,

through the thorn bush and cactus.

When traces of blood begin to mark your trail,

you'll begin to see something . . . maybe.

EDWARD ABBEY, *Desert Solitaire*

BETWEEN RIVER AND RIM

The terraced, travertine dams of the Little Colorado regularly flow cobalt blue and serve as the principal drainage of the Painted Desert.

Colors of spring emerge near the confluence with a flowering prickly pear cactus.

SOMETIME AFTER SECOND BREAKFAST, WHEN THE SUN STALLS directly overhead and commences to cook my brain, the birds go silent. Like all the desert souls, I too stop talking and revert inward to my sunburned thoughts. And then, as if a silent alarm sounds, small gusts of wind that feel like the breath of a furnace start kicking up miniature tornadoes of ancient dust.

"Damn, it's a cooker . . . hotter than hot today," I mumble.

I glance down at the thermostat on my pack while weaving between patches of beavertail cactus and clumps of agave spines woven among stubborn, bristly black brush. All of it seems harmoniously organized to claw at my legs. I'm surprised: the temperature reads only 94 degrees Fahrenheit. The line of dried salt on my faded blue shirt (my sweat meter) usually signifies temperatures over 100 degrees. Perhaps I'm just saltier today.

I clamber up onto an overhanging ledge at the base of a small bluff, seeking smoother travel. For a few hundred yards, I revel in brush-free hiking on a bench of sandstone whose surface is the color of apricot marmalade and gaze down at the Colorado River—that sinewy, brown ribbon of life for America's Southwest, quietly meandering some 2,500 feet below me. I refresh the map on my pocket GPS screen, squinting at the tiny blue dot signifying our location.

As feared, the dot isn't even close to where I'd hoped it would be. I crudely estimate eight miles to cross a network of three drainages—all littered with cliff bands and fractured rock—before we will hopefully arrive at our goal for the day: a series of small pools of glorious rainwater hidden in the shadows. Once there we can bed down in the rocks for

the night. We have already hoofed it some 10 miles today. Not bad, considering there is no trail in sight—unless you count the occasional tracks of bighorn, bobcat, raven, even rattlesnake.

I take a mental inventory: Four days of food. Some 75 miles to our next cache of nuts, freeze-dried meals, and cooking gas stashed by a rafting friend in a plastic bucket in a side canyon. Three dead camera batteries, two half-charged ones, and one is hooked to the solar panel on my pack. One and a half liters of water.

There is a saying experts often recite: "You are never walking toward water, only away from it." I try to ignore the sage advice, but it eddies in my head every day as the desert oven cooks the prior night's crisp air.

"How much water do you have left?" I blindly holler toward the rocks behind me.

No response. I stop and look back.

At first I see just heat waves rolling past an agave stalk shooting skyward. But then Kevin appears on a distant crimson ridge, some 100 yards back, his head down. I see he is speaking into his audio recorder, doing his diary update routine.

Whenever fatigue, thirst, or heat kick in, or the two of us have no more to discuss about the route—the beauty before us, the history beneath us, the memory of our lives in the world beyond the rims of the canyon—I look to the GPS or my camera, and Kevin turns to his words.

Kevin Fedarko has always been a writer, but to me he is also a trusted friend, despite the profound differences in our personalities. I seek action and adrenaline; he prefers silence. I am generally an optimist; he turns toward the darker side of things.

Nevertheless, we worked together as magazine journalists for years, and during this time we developed a friendship forged through the challenges of storytelling in the remote reaches of the world. But this current assignment for *National Geographic Magazine*—to hike the entire length of America's most iconic national park, the Grand Canyon—is the most audacious thing we've ever attempted.

On some level, it might also be the most foolhardy.

The clearest challenge we confront is the sheer scale and grandeur of this landscape. The Grand Canyon is 6,000 feet deep in places and more than 18 miles wide. It is so immense that it is the only canyon on earth visible from space. And because there are so many side canyons to traverse, our journey by foot will be significantly longer than merely floating down the 277-mile stretch of the Colorado River, the architect and inner highway of the canyon.

Atop the Redwall layer inside Marble Canyon, an agave cactus sends its stalk skyward just once in its life.

OVERLEAF
The calm waters inside Marble Canyon reflect the 335-million-year-old Redwall layer, known for its prominent, sheer cliffs.

Our trek will be more like 750 miles, roughly the length of California, and the elevation gain and loss required to negotiate its fractured landscape will be in the neighborhood of 100,000 vertical feet. Mount Everest rises more than 29,000 feet above sea level, so our hike is the equivalent of climbing multiple Himalayan peaks through a vertical desert plagued by 100-degree temperature swings, unstable rock, and long stretches with no water.

The second challenge is the route itself. For roughly 75 percent of the national park, there is simply no trail. As a result, more people have stood on the moon than have completed a continuous thru-hike of the Grand Canyon.

Beyond the daily physical challenge of staying alive, however, looms the larger goal of our journalistic transect, which involves documenting not only the magic of this landscape but also the ongoing challenges it faces as a result of being "loved to death" by the current generation of Americans before their children are able to enjoy it. That mission is proving harder than we ever expected, by several orders of magnitude.

Grand Canyon National Park is currently facing a storm of threats deriving from the growing popularity not only of the park itself, but also its neighboring landscapes under both federal and Native American jurisdiction. While the majority of these threats are tourist developments that offer the chance of economic prosperity for tribal lands, the impacts are poised to change the park's topography, its soundscape, and even its starry night sky.

These developments include a tram into the canyon floor with its very own restaurant, a bevy of new hotels on the rim, growing air tours, increased resource extraction, and all the human conveniences that follow. The politics behind each of these projects are as complex as the canyon itself, in many cases dividing tribal communities and creating negative impacts before the projects even start. Many canyon lovers, from tourists to tribal leaders, believe the park's beauty and resources are being auctioned off to the highest bidders.

Of course, this tug-of-war between conservation and entrepreneurial schemes designed to cash in on natural beauty isn't anything new. Proposals for the Grand Canyon—from damming the Colorado River to extracting the canyon's minerals—go back well before this geological marvel was listed as a national park. And many scars of those efforts remain today.

Hiking through the heart of this park is our way of taking an inventory of this iconic landscape while wrestling with a disturbing question: If we cannot protect this space, the seventh natural wonder of the world, what *can* we protect?

On this particularly hot afternoon, however, my mind is focused far less on photographing the landscape before me, and more on making miles to reach our next source of drinking water. I need to conserve energy (both for hiking and my camera). So I stop for a minute to let Kevin catch up.

I can tell by his breathiness that he is tired—exhausted.

As he approaches, he keeps talking into his recorder, his mind in a zone. He is talking about the dust and the grit of the canyon. "There is dirt everywhere," he says, panting. "It has crept under our fingernails and between our teeth and into the lines around our eyes—and on days like today, it feels as if the stuff has filtered into our veins and even now may be working its way into the chambers of our hearts."

I gaze out across the canyon and the buttes and the layers of time embedded in the sea of rock, and I realize that today Kevin is seeing more than I am.

Peering into the inner gorge from the Tonto bench triggers for many an overwhelming sense of wonder and humility.

FALL LEES FERRY TO BRIGHT ANGEL

We take our first steps downstream on a quiet morning, just two days before a full moon eclipse turns blood orange above the canyon's red wall. The Colorado River is flowing a pale turquoise green at just more than 8,200 cubic feet per second, a relatively average level for the fall. I'm already thinking of a swim, yet I'm all too aware that the alluring green of the river conceals its icy temperature.

Just a few miles upstream looms one of the canyon's bookends, Glen Canyon Dam, a remarkable piece of concrete engineering completed in 1966. Today it controls the flow of the river—releasing cold water from the depths of Lake Powell, which not only creates the rapids that river rafters dream of, but also spins the turbines below the dam that produce electrical current for the Southwest's power grid.

It's just a few hours after sunrise and the thermostat hanging on my pack already reads 84 degrees Fahrenheit. The forecast predicts it will break 100 degrees today. An unusually late heat wave is sweeping through the greater Grand Canyon area, reminding us that we are embarking on a thirsty adventure.

Kevin knows the journey ahead will be as challenging as it is beautiful. For years he worked inside this canyon as a river guide, rowing a baggage boat and learning firsthand how "the canyon respects no one." His experience became the research for a book about an infamous river runner named Kenton Grua, who also happened to be the first man to traverse the entirety of Grand Canyon National Park by foot—108 years after John Wesley Powell made his legendary expedition down the canyon's more obvious highway, the river.

We are on the heels of four experienced canyon explorers led by Rich Rudow. They are planning to keep walking until they reach Pearce Canyon, just shy of the Nevada border. They have kindly let Kevin and I tag along for two reasons. First, they know how quickly tourism is starting to change the park and they want to help us document it. But more importantly, they know we might need help finding the way. With no trail, moving downstream by foot is far from obvious.

The minute you leave the river, by even just a few hundred feet, you enter a different Grand Canyon—a world of secret labyrinths, mazes, ecological pockets of splendor, and one of the widest ranges of biodiversity in any national park in the United States, including Hawaii. Within hours of our departure, I stumble upon a condor feather. It is more than 18 inches long and one of many wildlife signs we spot on our nearly three-month journey stretched across the course of a year. For much of it, we learn to follow the thin, cliffy routes created by sheep or even wild horses and burros. Other times we follow the tracks of mountain lions and bobcats who know how to navigate the ledges better than anyone.

At certain side creeks and springs, endangered fish such as the speckled dace dart into the shadows below gurgling, champagne-like water. Although many bird species typically take flight in the fall to warmer regions, a handful that live in the Grand Canyon adjust their season by moving deeper into the canyon, choosing a lower rock layer to reside for winter. With 26 layers of rock—dropping more than a mile into the earth and dating back 1.7 billion years, or one-third of the

The Navajo Bridge on the eastern flank of Marble Canyon is the last active road visible from inside the park.

earth's age—to choose from, some species have evolved to chase seasons without leaving the canyon.

By our third day of moving by foot with all our supplies—including too many cameras and lenses on my back—I wish I too had wings to navigate this fractured, layered world.

It's around this point that Kevin and I begin to realize we cannot keep pace with the hiking team to which we have hitched our wagon. The temperature soars over 110 degrees and I wither into a state of cramps, heat exhaustion, and despair.

Even though I have spent years photographing the Colorado River, from its high mountains to the dusty delta where its flow now runs completely dry, I'm realizing the landscape of the Grand Canyon is like no other. Despite its overwhelming beauty, its enormity is quickly doing what it's famous for—dishing out a healthy dose of humility.

When we started out, I knew documenting this park, especially the complex development challenges around it, would be daunting. But by our sixth day of hiking, Kevin and I are shattered. Kevin's feet are encased in blisters and many look infected. My heel is missing most of its skin and is so infected it looks like someone fired at it with a miniature shotgun, but it goes mostly unnoticed because the cramps running through my body, like a mouse squirming under my skin, are consuming the last of my focus. My vision shrinks, and I sense I'm on the verge of unconsciousness. At first I think it is heatstroke but later learn I'm suffering from hyponatremia—a condition of low body salt that is the leading cause of death in the canyon.

It is clear to everyone that we need help and will have to exit. The next day we slowly climb and crawl some 3,200 vertical feet up an Ancestral Puebloan route at North Canyon to lick our psychological and physical wounds. Our friend J. P. Clark, notified by satellite text message, hikes in to meet us with hydration salts, usher us out, and give us a ride back to civilization where we will reassess our entire plan. Part of me wonders if we should quit completely.

Three weeks later, however, we return, thanks to a community of canyon lovers who push us past our intimidation and back into the depths. They assure us that with less equipment and better planning we will learn to listen to the canyon and read its complexities better. Reluctantly, we descend back in, this time with two canyon veterans, Mathieu Brown and Kelly McGrath, who have joined us to hike to the confluence of the Little Colorado and main Colorado Rivers—a place on many people's minds. Harlan Taney, another canyon guru, meets us later with a resupply of food and good spirit.

Glen Canyon Dam is a technological marvel upstream of the Grand Canyon on its eastern flank. It unnaturally regulates the water flow of the Colorado River inside the canyon.

A forgotten drain (above) and ladder (opposite) serve as stark reminders of another era when construction workers once resided atop the Redwall layer in the 1940s, poised to build the Marble Canyon Dam.

For six days we move roughly 12 to 14 miles a day, weaving our way atop the Redwall, a layer of limestone where industrial debris from the Marble Canyon Dam exploration site quietly petrifies some 1,200 feet above the river. It is a stark reminder of how quickly conservation views and values can change.

Now carrying just one camera and one lens, I start to meditate on the differences between what we want and what we need. Photographically, my entire journey ahead will be a lesson in simplicity, patience, and minimalism. The canyon will be the teacher.

By early November, after climbing and descending enough to make our knees ache, we reach the confluence. The Hopi, Zuni, and Navajo tribes—and others—believe this location, where the emerald

waters of the male Colorado River meet the turquoise flow of the Little Colorado, marks the point where life begins.

It is the first among a group of developments that are threatening to change this canyon's wilderness area. We leave the boundary of the national park just beyond the confluence and spend nine hours hiking 3,200 vertical feet to the rim—the location of a proposed gondola called the Grand Canyon Escalade, a project whose backers predict it could deliver up to 10,000 people a day to the sacred mixing waters below. In light of the fact that 26,000 people float through the canyon in a year, the tram would eclipse the annual visitation to the site in just three days.

When we reach the rim at the location of the project's proposed hotel complex, tired and sweaty, we are met by a group of Navajo elders, mostly women, including Renae Yellowhorse. As part of an organization called Save the Confluence, she has been quietly fighting the project. Over homemade mutton stew on the flat, brushy world above the canyon, Renae tells us they don't want to "see Disneyland" at the rim of their "church."

After a week inside the vertical depths of the canyon, the horizontal realm of the rim is arresting. Many of the women we meet have spent their entire lives here raising sheep. For most of them, Navajo is their first and only language. Although the developer behind the Grand Canyon Escalade, a non-Navajo resident from Phoenix, promises to boost the troubled Navajo economy, the Save the Confluence women raise a host of objections ranging from security and light pollution to fresh water access, pollution, crowding, and cultural exploitation.

"We understand economic growth," they say, "but just not here."

As the sun sets across the confluence above the north rim of the canyon, I look downstream. We have more than 500 miles of hiking left to reach our goal.

By then, perhaps I'll better understand how to move through and document the wonder of the world these Navajo women have gazed upon their entire lives.

Rich in calcium carbonate from Blue Spring, the turquoise-colored Little Colorado River is the longest tributary of the Grand Canyon.

OVERLEAF
Traveling by foot for days, chasing the sun, and navigating ledges that rival skyscrapers offers a perspective measured in scale and silence.

PREVIOUS SPREAD
Moving downriver requires piecing together a puzzle of thin ledges and cliffs (left) through a labyrinth of rock, time, and beauty (right).

The springs that trickle life into slot canyons (opposite) sustain a remarkably wide range of biodiversity, including tarantulas (above).

OVERLEAF
The source of life in the canyon is the water that collects in potholes (left) hidden in the shadows throughout the many tributaries (right).

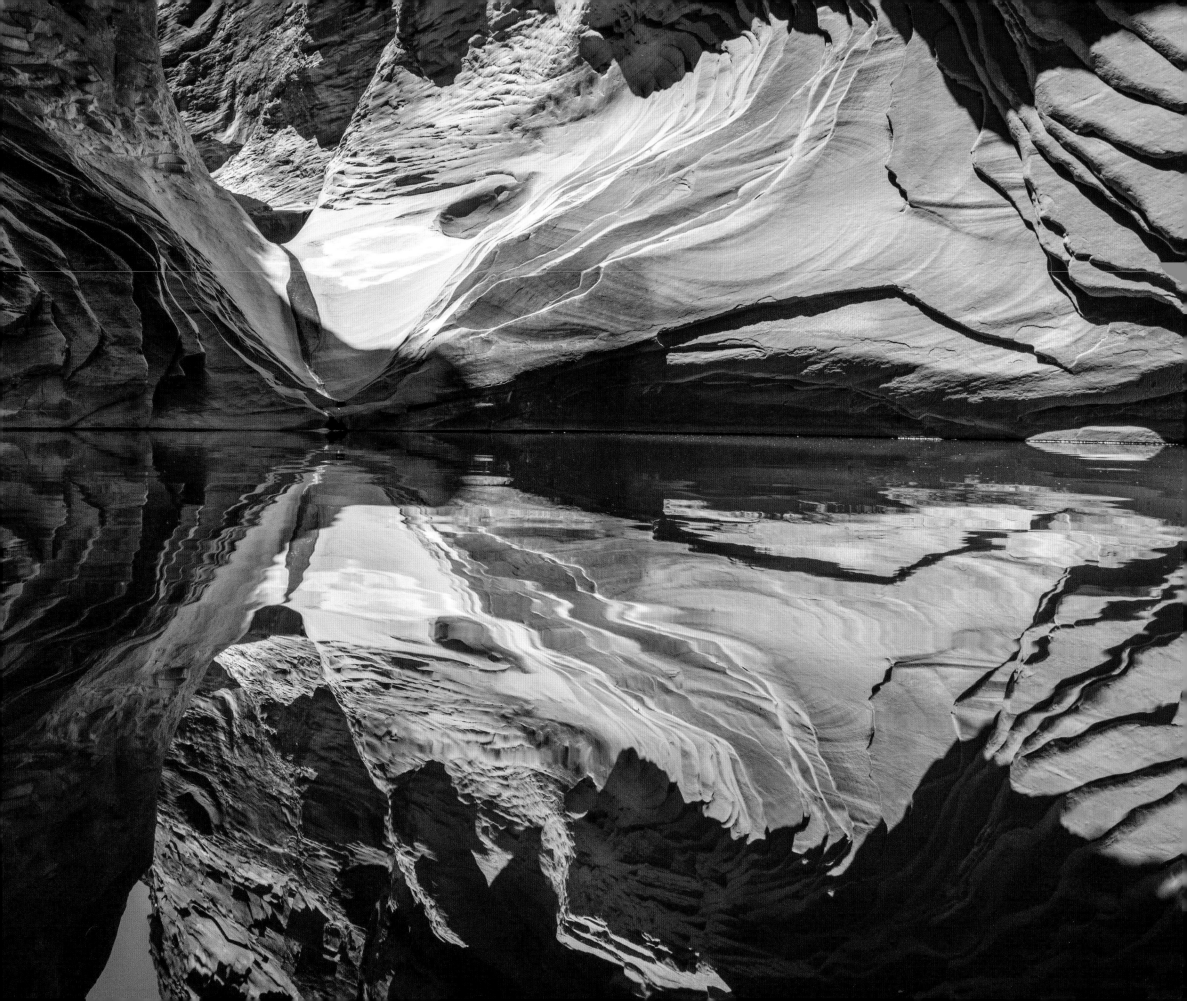

PREVIOUS SPREAD
Slot canyons can serve as escalators through millions of years of geologic time, allowing access to the river, the main highway through the park.

The granite cliffs of the inner gorge, mostly impassable by foot, line the Colorado River through the central corridor as sunrise highlights a distant wildfire haze.

OVERLEAF
Vasey's Paradise emerges from the Redwall cliffs, releasing water from the north rim that originates miles away (left). Much of the water in the canyon is supplied by rainwater captured in ever-changing potholes (right).

Distant rainstorms generate flash floods miles
upstream that change the vibrant turquoise flow of
the Little Colorado to the color of chocolate milk.

The sacred overlook on the Navajo Nation's land
above the confluence has served as a place of
prayer for many. A tram development, if approved,
would originate at this location and carry thousands
of visitors a day 3,200 vertical feet below.

A setting sun highlights a dying 15-foot agave stalk
near the Beamer Trail (left), where the shadow of
the author frames the route (right).

A Rocky Mountain toad, one of 10 amphibian species in the park, enjoys a swim (above). From the air, the Little Colorado can be seen merging with the main Colorado River on the right (opposite).

OVERLEAF
According to Hopi mythology, certain springs that flow up into the Little Colorado River canyon are where life emerged.

Below the confluence, the canyon yawns open into small floodplains and vegetation, such as coyote willow, arrowweed, seep willow, western honey mesquite, catclaw acacia, and invasive tamarisk.

The Escalante Trail winds past Unkar Creek, an area rich with Ancestral Puebloan archaeology.

OVERLEAF
The route meanders miles around side drainages, crossing millions of years of geologic time yet only moving a few hundred yards downstream.

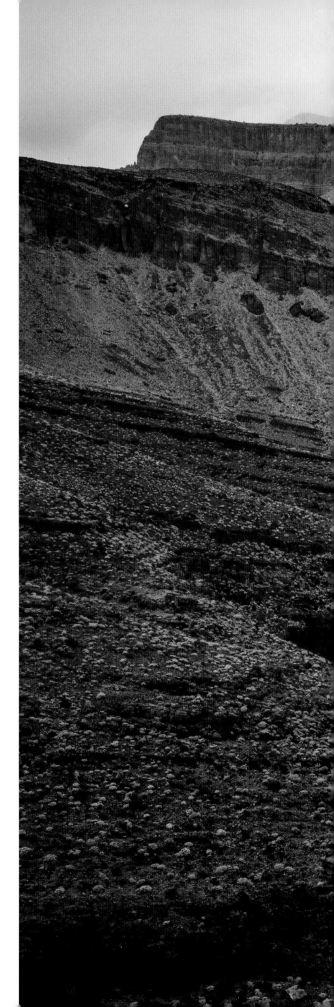

Looking upstream into the inner gorge at night reveals
the canyon's second river, the celestial river of stars.

OVERLEAF
A fall rain shower dances across the Tonto bench as
the Colorado River descends through the charcoal-
colored walls of the inner gorge.

Autumn begins to color a cottonwood in a tributary of the south rim.

OVERLEAF
Etched graffiti from the early 1900s serves as a reminder that the notion to "leave it as it is" is an ongoing challenge (left). Meanwhile, the canyon's main architect continues its work, slowly carving through the 1.7 billion-year-old Vishnu schist granite below (right).

A molten light reflects the canyon walls in a rainwater pothole (above). Looking roughly 2,500 feet upward at the south rim, hundreds of millions of years of geologic time can be witnessed in one view (opposite).

OVERLEAF
Upriver from the central corridor, mist clings to the south rim.

Cottonwoods define the beauty of Indian Garden on the Bright Angel Trail, home to the Havasupai people before the canyon became a national park (opposite). Six species of rattlesnake reside throughout the Grand Canyon. We kept a keen eye while hiking, but we saw very few (above).

WINTER BRIGHT ANGEL TO HAVASU

SOMETIME AROUND 4:00 P.M., AS AN AUBURN DECEMBER LIGHT stretches shadows across the canyon, I stop walking—certain that someone, or something, is watching me. I scan the sandstone rib on the alcove ahead of me . . . nothing. At least nothing I can see. But some ancient, long-forgotten survival sense, more awakened now after 40 days of hiking some 350 miles across this desert landscape, is speaking to me. And it keeps quietly telling me that something out there is eyeing me.

That something, at least in my mind, is a mountain lion, a large one, whose tracks we've been following for days. Thoughts of becoming lunch aside, I'm actually thrilled when I locate another paw track because this canyon resident seems to know the way through the ribbons of rock ledges and cliffs of the ocher-tinted Esplanade bench when there is otherwise no trail or marker to follow. And the last thing we need is to get lost out here or pinned atop a 2,000-foot cliff amid the Redwall formation.

Throughout the late fall and early winter, we've moved more than 100 miles downstream on the Beamer, Escalante, and Tonto Trails lining the south side of the canyon. This old network of dirt pathways varies between assiduously maintained and half forgotten, but it offers the only route, aside from wildlife tracks, that we experience throughout the entire canyon. Even an old, overgrown trail feels like a pedestrian highway compared to our usual bushwhacking.

As we move into the long, cold nights of January, we climb 1,500 feet—roughly 200 million years in geologic time—to the Esplanade, where pockets of rainwater are more consistent. But the route is much less so. From our lofty perch, the Colorado River winds more than a half mile below us, a shimmering ribbon of silver and blue.

Long before I shouldered a pack on this mission, I did another photographic project that involved studying the entirety of the canyon's primary architect. For the better part of two years, I followed the Colorado River from its source in the Rocky Mountains all the way to its historic terminus at the Sea of Cortez in Mexico. I was alarmed to learn that "the most loved and litigated river in the world" no longer reaches the ocean. But now, from the perspective atop some of these myriad layers of rock and time, the fragility of the Southwest's lifeline becomes more evident.

Toward the end of January, we approach the Great Thumb Mesa, a giant geologic digit that juts north some 20 miles, pushing the canyon and the river on a giant northerly arc. There are few exits or breaks in the rim here. Moreover, even if you can scramble your way out of the canyon itself, the land above, which belongs to the Havasupai tribe, is reserved for hunting, so there are no roads that are accessible in the winter.

Escaping the canyon's grip by rappelling some 3,000 feet down to the river is equally challenging, and there are few floating the river this time of year. Remote is an understatement. In essence, we are pinned on a 300-million-year-old layer of Hermit Shale that readily crumbles into the void below. Welcome to the wilds of wilderness, where a lion is your guide.

Each time we cross the many drainages that pinch into the cliffs, closing the door of routes forward, this lion, whose tracks keep appearing fresh with detail, shows us the way. After four days of shadowing the cat's trail, however, I start questioning whether our feline friend is guiding or stalking us.

The terraced step of earth's history is seen from the Tonto bench.

OVERLEAF
Winter brings shorter days, colder temperatures, and storms that can shroud the canyon in snow.

Thankfully, our friend Rich Rudow, who is fresh off completing his own 58-day continuous thru-hike (making him the ninth person in recorded history to complete a thru-hike of the Grand Canyon), has decided to join us because he knows the challenges of this perilous section of the canyon.

For this particular stretch, roughly 170 miles, Kelly McGrath and Amy Martin are also joining us. With just one cache of food stored by the river 120 miles downstream, we need help shouldering 10 days of food, extra gas, winter gear, and climbing equipment.

We have learned firsthand that heavy packs can thwart plans. Kelly and Amy are extremely experienced hiking in the canyon, but neither has ever hiked this particular cliffy maze. Both are excited to experience this hard-to-reach wilderness, one they have only gazed up at while floating past during their time working as river guides.

During the final days of January, a wind picks up from the south and an angry mass of dark clouds fills our expansive view. Rain starts to lightly spit and then blast the crimson rocks. Everything around us quickly starts to shimmer. The muted gray brush glistens jet black. Under a lightweight tarp and tent, we hunker in for what a satellite text warns us could be the storm of the winter.

Sometime around midnight, the sound of wind combined with the rattle of "male rain," a Navajo term for extreme downpours, becomes muffled. Then it softens.

Snow.

For the next 24 hours, ice pellets followed by fluffy flakes fill our world. The temperature plummets, like a rock slab cascading off the edge, and everything freezes.

I sleep wearing two down jackets and every other layer I'm carrying. I tuck my camera batteries into my armpits—a photographer's plea with the canyon to prevent my camera from dying. Our shoes and water bottles, despite being nestled at the feet of our sleeping bags, turn into bricks of ice.

Kevin looks at me with the fading hint of a smile and says, "When do we call the rescue . . . now?"

I nervously laugh. Getting help in this remote corner of our famed national park is not easy. Even if a helicopter could land on the sloped ledges next to the cliffs where we are perched, the snowy whiteout prevents it. A rescue is out of the question.

Nevertheless, the photographer in me is thrilled to see this world of red and brown and pink suddenly framed with white. It becomes a black-and-white dream. Negative space takes over. At the same time, we

all know that hiking on 45- and 50-degree slopes, which are coated with wet icy snow and crumble into the abyss below, is far from ideal. Quietly, we all ponder Kevin's question: How are we going to get out of here?

Since hiking up provides no easier options and turning around would require more days of backtracking than our food supply can support, we trudge on. For two days, we cling to side hills with frozen feet and hands as fear rattles inside our chests. We also move across some of the most striking country I suspect I will ever lay eyes on. The juxtaposition haunts me. The more the canyon challenges us, the more I'm captivated by its beauty. I stop so frequently to frame images, always removing my gloves, that eventually one gets caught by the wind, flutters into the white, and vanishes over the cliff. The price of remote winter photography.

At the height of the storm, we follow Rich into Owl Eyes Bay, a place defined by two enormous, hollowed-out caverns looming below the rim. They are so colossal one can see them miles upstream even from the river. They perfectly resemble the eyes of a slightly haunted owl, staring at you no matter where you are.

With crampon-like spikes attached to our shoes to keep us from slipping into the abyss to our right, we still slide and slip. The micro-spikes keep balling up with snow and ice, making traction even worse. Carefully moving now through nearly a foot of snow, we focus on every single step. We all know a single misstep could be our last.

A hiking friend of Rich, Ioana Hociota, passed through here in February 2012. There was no snow at the time, yet she mysteriously and tragically slipped. Unable to stop herself, she tumbled down a short ravine and whisked off the edge, some 300 feet down the Redwall layer, before crashing through the canopy of a cottonwood grove below. At just 24 years old, Ioana had degrees in mathematics and biology, spoke four languages, and loved the challenge of traveling through this wild, unpredictable rocky realm as much as she enjoyed running ultramarathons or writing poetry. She had hiked the entire length of the Grand Canyon, except for this bay. It was her last.

Forced to move slower, we sleep in the heart of Owl Eyes Bay on a nearly flat bench covered in snow, not far from where Ioana fell. Rich offers a tearful tribute to his friend, then we all crawl into our tents and our thoughts for the night. The temperature drops to eight degrees Fahrenheit (minus eight on the rim), and when we awake, once again our water, shoes, and parts of our souls are frozen.

We melt snow for coffee and pour boiling water over our shoes. It is a desperate attempt to thaw them so our feet can slip in. We are

Layered light filters over the terrain we traversed by foot in the fall.

OVERLEAF
A January sunrise lights up Huxley Terrace and the South Bass Trail.

eager to move. A sliver of sun beckons us on the far shoulder of the bay. Due to the slower pace of unexpectedly hiking in snow, we will go at least one day without food, maybe more.

Oddly, amid the mental and physical stress, I awake with a sharper appreciation of the canyon and its beauty. Perhaps it's the snow, the hunger, or the combination of it all, but I start noticing more details around us: tracks, insects, birds, more energy-efficient hiking routes.

Compared to Amy, however, I see little. Despite hiking with an injured, badly inflamed, and twisted knee from a simple slip, Amy spots archaeological wonders by the dozens—which we all blindly stroll past. Arrowheads, potsherds, a spear tip that she estimates to be more than 12,000 years old. Despite our sense of isolation, we are not the first humans to travel this landscape.

And like our Ancestral Puebloan predecessors who sought food here, we too are motivated by hunger and must keep moving. By the first of February, we are rappelling into Olo Canyon and marveling at the dance of light on the springs that magically gurgle from the rock. I'm so captivated by this polished natural plumbing system that I'm reluctant to keep moving for fear that I'll miss the photographic moment of my life, but my stomach protests.

It is remarkable how giddy and elated one can become when one is calorie deprived and arrives at a bucket of freeze-dried . . . well, anything. Amid uncontrolled hoots of joy and laughter, we locate our stash and promptly devour our most coveted snacks—mostly chocolate—giggling and screaming like candy-crazed kids at a piñata party.

The next morning, we return to following the tracks of our furry friends. Our mountain lion is gone, so we turn to the bighorn sheep, which offers the key to unlocking lines through the Muav and Redwall layers of cliffs and crevasses that look impassable. If we can locate their poop, or what we call "black nuggets of gold," we know we have a way forward. Or, at least, we know an agile-footed, four-legged, canyon-born sheep has made it through the overhanging, stomach-dropping ledge before us (without a pack of course).

In some stretches of the park closer to the rim, we also find elk, deer, and coyote tracks, plus the odd hoofprints of wild horses that once meandered off the rim of the Havasupai Reservation and now call the national park home. Six hundred feet below the Esplanade live wild burros, which were abandoned by miners and explorers and have stubbornly eked out livings despite the National Park Service's effort to relocate them. Unlike the mules, the horse tracks are hard to follow and often hard to see (we eye six horses). But their canyon

wisdom consistently helps us find not only routes but also potholes of rain and snow water.

By mid-February, we spend hours discussing how the future of the canyon will be and currently is being written on the rims above us. As the Grand Canyon Escalade tram proposal is debated on the Navajo lands to the east of us, another development not far to the southeast is discussed in the halls of federal agencies.

Near the canyon's entrance town of Tusayan, Arizona, a mega-resort boasting millions of square feet of commercial space and thousands of homes is proposed. Like the tram, it divides many. And once again, water, or the lack thereof, is at the center of the debate.

As we reach the blue-green waters of Havasu Creek, we hike up the drainage, out of the park, and past a network of picturesque waterfalls to the Havasupai village of Supai. We are all weathered and skinny, but glowing from our time soaked in silence, simplicity, and self-sufficiency. We are also excited to taste our first real meal and have a hot shower. If you exclude snow showers, it will be our first in almost three weeks.

Not long after we leave the canyon, I talk to Carletta Tilousi, a council member of the Havasupai tribe. With just 800 members, the tribe's greatest fear is water contamination or shortage, Carletta tells me. Havasu Creek erupts inside Havasu Canyon by Supai, like so many of the springs we have witnessed. There is clearly an intricate web of springs that connect the water table, and Carletta says, "Whatever happens on the top affects below." She fears that any future developments for tourism or mines will either dry up their scarce water supply or inadvertently pollute it.

Like the Ancestral Puebloans who resided throughout the canyon, the Havasupai people lived in and around the Grand Canyon long before it became a national park. I heed Carletta's advice. Kevin and I have some 250 more miles to complete our journey—and every mile depends on the water holes we will find inside.

The falls in Havasu Creek define this southern tributary, home to the Havasupai tribe, "the people of the blue-green waters."

OVERLEAF
From the south rim of Forster Canyon, dawn lights the layer cake of deep time and the river stretch known as Conquistador Aisle.

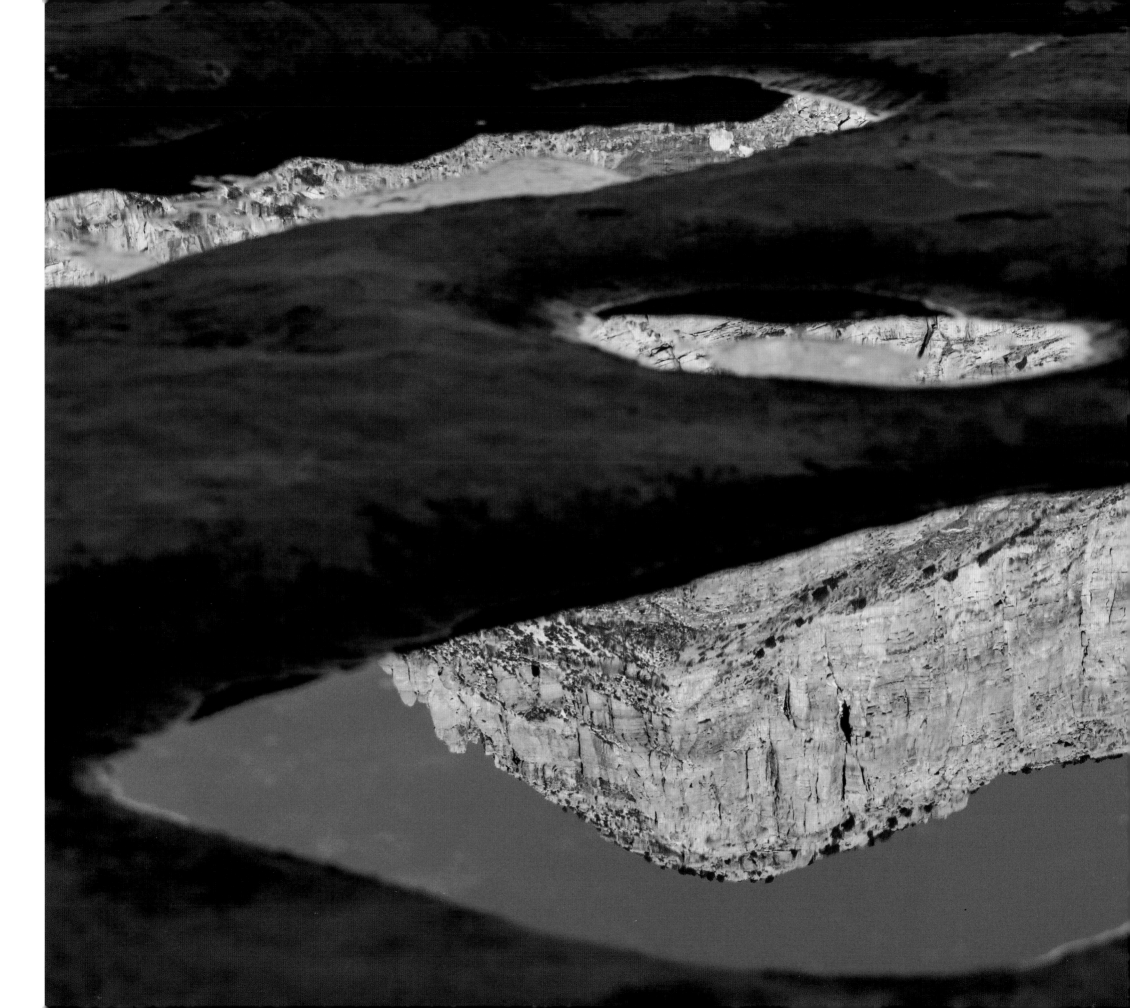

Winter brings freezing temperatures and
potholes brimming with snowmelt.

OVERLEAF
Cacti such as the beavertail turn shades of
deep purple in the winter months.

The last kiss of light dots the north rim (opposite) as the river below reflects the glow (above).

OVERLEAF
The Esplanade ledge, 1,500 feet below the rim, offers a contemplative view of the canyon and Powell Plateau to the north.

A pothole oasis reflects a dying pinyon pine, one of 200 species of trees and shrubs inside the Grand Canyon.

OVERLEAF
Like the pages of a book, a side canyon opens up on the north rim (left). A waning moon hangs onto dusk light, mirrored in thin pools of snowmelt below (right).

Wild horses—runaways from the Havasupai
Reservation lands on the rim above—roam the
Esplanade ledge around the Great Thumb Mesa.

OVERLEAF
The circular patterns of a yucca cactus (left)
create their own scale near the entrance to
Olo Canyon (right).

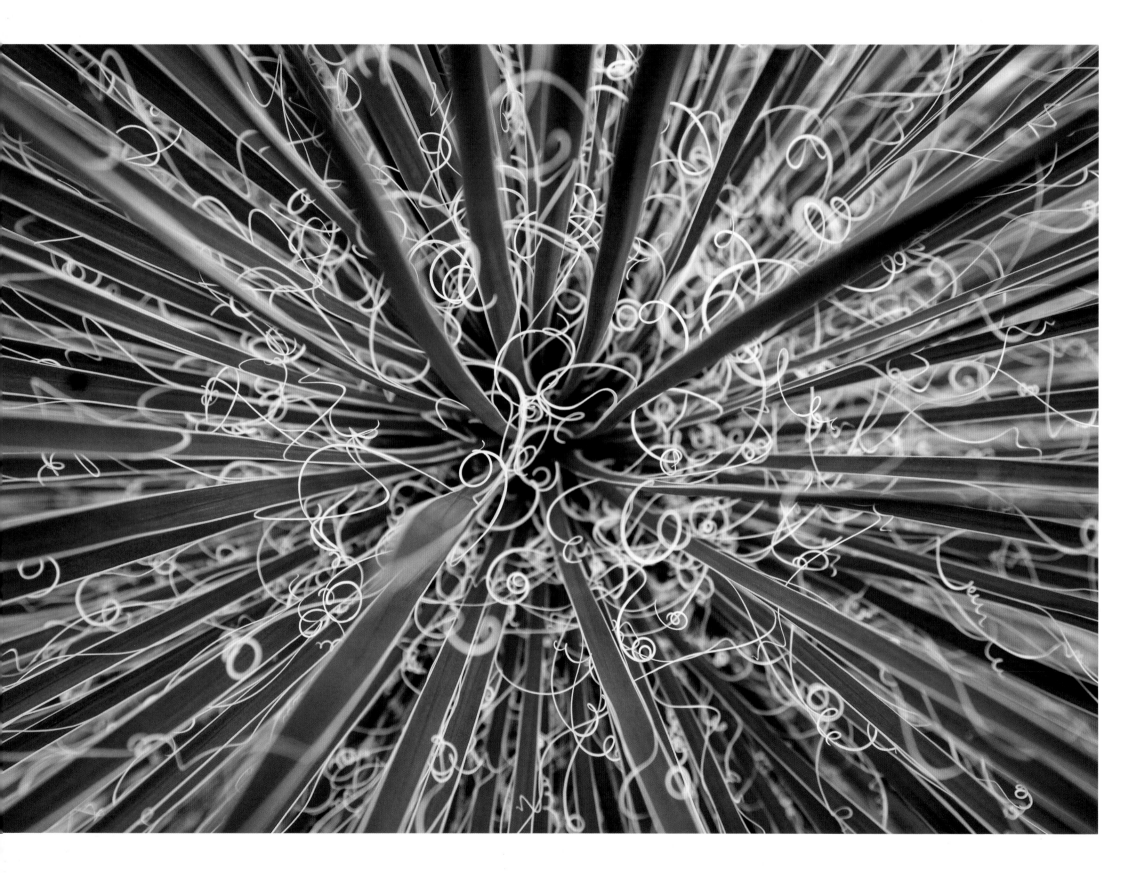

The Great Thumb Mesa juts into the canyon, pushing the Colorado River—and hikers with it—miles north in a giant arc.

OVERLEAF
Pinyon pine trees appear miniature in size in relation to their cliffy home between the Redwall limestone and Coconino sandstone layers (left). Horn Creek, a drainage on the south rim, appears pristine, but the abandoned Orphan Mine above it—which prospected for uranium until 1969—continues to contaminate its water beyond safe drinking standards (right).

Navigating the ledges of the canyon often requires using wildlife tracks. There are more than 90 species of mammals that call Grand Canyon National Park home.

OVERLEAF
Winter storms can quickly turn sloped terrain into icy ramps above the thousands of feet of terraced ledges below.

PREVIOUS SPREAD
A two-day storm is broken by a beam of light
glinting across the canyon walls near Tapeats Creek.

Melting snow and cracking ice can create a
symphony of sounds as the canyon erodes.

OVERLEAF
Freezing temperatures quickly return in the
evening, as does a blanket of winter silence (left).
When the storm clears, winter temperatures
create a crisp clarity witnessed by the intensity
of the night sky (right).

PREVIOUS SPREAD
Olo Canyon serves as a sublime subway system through sculpted layers of limestone that lead to the basement of the canyon.

Following sheep droppings helped us navigate the Muav limestone benches.

OVERLEAF
Due to the remarkable verticality across the canyon's western reaches (left), the only way down to the river requires technical rope work (right).

The silence inside slot canyons can be so dense
that the shuffle of feet or clatter of sheep hooves
can be heard hundreds of yards away.

OVERLEAF
At certain layers in the rock, fresh water emerges
and then vanishes (left). The maze of water
below the surface of the canyon and park is as
complicated as the topography above (right).

Sunshine in the winter is a cherished, welcome friend.

OVERLEAF
Located north of Havasu Creek, Mount Synella serves
as a beacon to the western Grand Canyon and is
believed to be sacred by the Havasupai tribe.

The mineral-rich, turquoise waters of Havasu Creek stairstep down travertine dams on the Havasupai Reservation.

OVERLEAF
A cottonwood leaf (left) becomes part of the runoff below Mooney Falls (right), predominantly fed by underground water sources.

SPRING 150-MILE CANYON TO DIAMOND CREEK

After nearly two months of hiking, we cross the Grand Canyon-Parashant National Monument on the north rim and a new track appears, something I don't expect. An ATV. Two miles later, we meet two buddies out on an overnight. When they see us, they look a bit startled, ashen even. They reveal that due to the remoteness of our location, they thought we might have been survivors of an airplane crash.

Apparently, we look a bit beat up and rattled. Bushwhacking 15 to 24 miles a day can do that.

The farther we march west, now on the north side of the river because we are denied a permit to cross the Hualapai tribal lands on the south, it becomes obvious that despite our remoteness and solitude (the ATV guys are the eighth and ninth humans we've encountered in 600 miles of hiking), there *has* been human activity across this landscape for thousands of years—from mastodon hunters and miners to dam builders and ragged hikers.

The western Grand Canyon is vast and then some. As a result, those who know it sometimes refer to the place as "the Godscape." The endless buttes, wind-sculpted ribs, and mazes of side drainages, some of which are so large they could easily qualify as entire parks in their own right, create a greater sense of awe and smallness.

At night, when we stop our constant motion, we hear the back-and-forth hoots of owls cutting a silence so deep I can only describe it as a liquid that floods our ears and everything around us. Occasionally, the bleating of bighorn sheep, thousands of feet below us, float into our open-aired camp as we watch the celestial tracks of stars (and satellites) above us until our eyelids give way to fatigue.

The cold and snow of winter have now melted into the lengthening days of March. To save weight, Kevin and I are carrying just a rain tarp and more food. As long as we can find water, we can bend our bodies to sleep in nearly any rocky depression. It's amazing how comfortable a slab of sandstone can feel after hiking for 12 hours.

Despite my fatigue, I often lay awake at night: sometimes too wired and worried about finding water and sometimes too spellbound by the spray of stars above us. Kevin describes this celestial sweep as a second river—one that mirrors the main Colorado below us.

Being inside the only canyon on the planet that can be seen from space makes you feel miniscule. And when you stare skyward, you realize one of this landscape's unspoken marvels is the clarity of its night sky—one of the few landscapes in America without a blanket of light pollution. I lose myself in the space above and the idea that Mother Nature is still queen in some parts.

As I doze, I overhear Kevin taking audio notes (easier than writing when he is tired), remarkably 100 yards from me. It is so quiet I think he is five feet away. He describes these moments "below the river of stars" as if "the canyon is holding us in the palm of its hand."

It dawns on me that two of the greatest treasures we have encountered in this landscape are not easily captured with digital pixels and cameras.

The first is auditory. When you get beyond the roar of the river inside the canyon, the silence is so profound and so ancient that it escapes description. At times it makes my ears ring because I'm trying to listen so hard to something that isn't there. At other times the void

On the north rim atop 150-Mile Canyon, a fence is a flashback to the area's cattle ranching history before the national park expanded in 1975.

OVERLEAF
The Dome reflects in a shallow pool of stillness.

of noise is so profound I wonder if it belongs to another world—a world we have long forgotten.

In the evenings or early mornings, Kevin and I can converse in relaxed, tired voices even though we are the length of a football field apart. The same occurs when we hike, but if a single rib of rock separates us, we can't hear each other holler at the top of our lungs, as if, at times, our voices can't pierce the blanket of quiet that envelops us. It creates a wondrous and sometimes nerve-racking world of quiet.

The second treasure that feels as fragile as the umbrella of emptiness around us is the unfiltered and undiluted night sky. The clarity of Kevin's "river of stars" is hemmed on the edges by the distant glow of Las Vegas and St. George, Utah. Otherwise, looking across the sweep of erosion, rock, and time, there is no sign of civilization before us. Of course, we do see jets blinking above, mostly headed to Los Angeles, but they die down after midnight.

Days earlier, we witnessed ancient paintings in a secret cavern. And not far from it, we collected water from tiny potholes just below a Puebloan roasting pit. The multicolored paintings are said to be 4,000 years old. Some argue older.

I ponder how these ancient canyon dwellers most likely gazed on the same vastness, trying to understand it and their place in it. The thought typically makes me feel tiny—even irrelevant—not with a sense of futility, but more awe and wonder. I feel lucky to be so immersed in such an ancient, unchanged world.

Some days we find centimeter-deep potholes from which we use syringes to painstakingly pull the last water. Other days, we find only cracked earth where rainwater had collected earlier, but already evaporated into the arid sky. And each day, I try to find new ways to photograph the beauty around us. Considering this park is the most photographed canyon in the world, fighting redundant, cliché imagery plagues my mind as much as our hunt for water.

Kevin and I are alone, but Rich Rudow, all too aware of the dangerous water game we are playing, sends us satellite text messages with coordinates to suspected potholes that I check twice a day. But even when we get updates, Rich's information isn't always accurate since the water puzzle changes daily, hourly even. Two of his most reliable water locations prove dated and filled with dust, forcing us to become entirely dependent on our ability to read the landscape—and luck—to survive.

The story of water in and around the canyon is remarkably complex and mysterious. While water, wind, and time are the real artists

behind the textured rock canvas, there is little known about how it works. As I attempt to visually capture the complexity of this artery-like network, I'm once again drawn further toward the microworlds at my feet.

Water travels through layers of rock, hard and soft, meandering laterally and vertically through cracks, crevasses, tunnels, and caves. Some of the softer geological layers soak up water like a sponge. But eventually, water emerges somewhere in the canyon—bubbling up in the form of a spring or dripping seep—as it tries to reach the Colorado River.

A park hydrologist named Ben Tobin once placed florescent dye in sinkholes scattered on the Kaibab Plateau on the north rim. Researchers later checked the springs and creeks to see where the dye emerged. One seep, located on the north rim to the east of where we started hiking, surprised everyone.

Based on prior research, experts assumed the colored dye would logically flow downstream. It didn't. Remarkably, it traveled 24 horizontal miles and dropped 6,000 vertical feet. Traces of the dye showed up in a series of springs, such as Vasey's Paradise in Marble Canyon to the east, and Deer Creek, Thunder River, and Tapeats Creek hundreds of miles to the west.

There are two main aquifers in the canyon, the Redwall and the Coconino, which sit above it. It is believed they are connected, but experts admit there is little understanding beyond that.

On an overcast morning, Kevin and I walk up a slot canyon, where we are delighted and surprised to find water behind a small concrete dam. Above the dam I notice old mining debris: steel wheels, cables, piles of rock. Without much thought, I guzzle my last bottle and happily fill my empties with the clear, silt-free water. We treat the aqua for bacteria and then move on.

Roughly 800 feet above the head of the slot canyon, we come across the Copper Mountain Mine and another swath of debris. We are in the Grand Canyon-Parashant National Monument, which was established in January 2000, transferring roughly one million acres of land from the Bureau of Land Management into the hands of the National Park Service. Prior to that, ranchers and miners explored this remote northern reach of the Grand Canyon. We are now hoofing it through the rusted reminders of who came before.

At the entrance to a side shaft, a sign reads: DANGER HIGH RADIATION AREA. Just uphill of the shaft are signs of an abandoned operation: pumps, pipes, rods, an upside-down vehicle, a collapsing lean-to shed, a cook stove, and a swath of rusty cans, gears, boxes riddled with bullet holes, 50-gallon drums, and hoses.

"What do you think of that water we just gulped and loaded up with?" I ask Kevin.

He laughs while looking distressed.

"Yeah, not great, but do we have a better option . . . or any option right now? That was the first water we've seen in miles."

Evidence of mining in and around the canyon exists in patches in the park. As we hike, we occasionally see it, but the impacts resonate long after we move on. Three hundred miles upstream, we had crossed Horn Creek on the south side of the canyon, and although we were thirsty, we kept walking without filling our bottles. The park warns visitors not to drink from Horn Creek because of uranium contamination that exceeds Environmental Protection Agency (EPA) standards.

Debris from the abandoned Copper Mountain Mine in Grand Canyon-Parashant National Monument remains scattered around the landscape. Companies prospected for uranium here in the 1950s and '60s (opposite). A uranium mine is seen from the air on the north rim of the Grand Canyon outside of the national park (above).

Much of that contamination originates from the orphan mine on the rim next to the park headquarters. Opened in 1893 to mine copper, the orphan mine officially started producing uranium in 1951. It went on to produce more than 4.2 million pounds of uranium oxide, plus copper, silver, and other minerals. The estimated value of the uranium alone comes in at $40 million.

Today, the orphan mine has been mostly reclaimed after closing in the late 1960s, except for the water below it. In 1995, a research team led by hydrologist David Kreamer of the University of Nevada-Las Vegas measured uranium levels of Horn Creek, the drainage below the mine, and 15 other springs and found them to be above EPA drinking water standards.

Under the fear of water contamination, new uranium exploration around the park was put under a 20-year moratorium by the federal government in 2012. Current mining operations were grandfathered in to continue business as usual, and today the mining industry is lobbying to lift the ban.

Between our hiking journeys, I visit the Canyon Mine just south of the park headquarters, the only operational mine near the Grand Canyon, to document and better understand the issue. Curtis Moore with Energy Fuels says the uranium ore is "the best in the Southwest" and the company operates under the strictest environmental regulations in the world. Moore also sees uranium as a job producer and clean fuel for the future. He adds, "It's also the least understood. People hear uranium and they get nervous."

Days after my visit, a group of 20 Havasupai tribal members perform a protest outside the mine's fence surrounding the property.

"We are the front lines of a water contamination situation," says Carletta Tilousi, a tribal council member. She fears the 1,500-foot mine shaft may eventually hit groundwater, contaminate it, and ultimately find its way to Havasu Creek, much like the researchers' dye.

Others warn that playing roulette with water in the Grand Canyon is not worth the risk. When dealing with such an important place and the Southwest's drinking water, there is too much at stake, they say.

Hiking now on the Esplanade ledge far above the river, we leave the Copper Mountain Mine and its littered history behind. We carry our fill of water, hoping it's not heavily contaminated.

Spring temperatures continue to rise, and our ability to find water inversely drops. I start questioning if it is worth risking our survival to keep going. We are around 100 miles from the northwest border of the park, but there is no value if we perish while trying to reach it.

Havasupai tribal members protest uranium mining outside the Canyon Mine, currently an active mine located just three miles from the south rim entrance to Grand Canyon National Park.

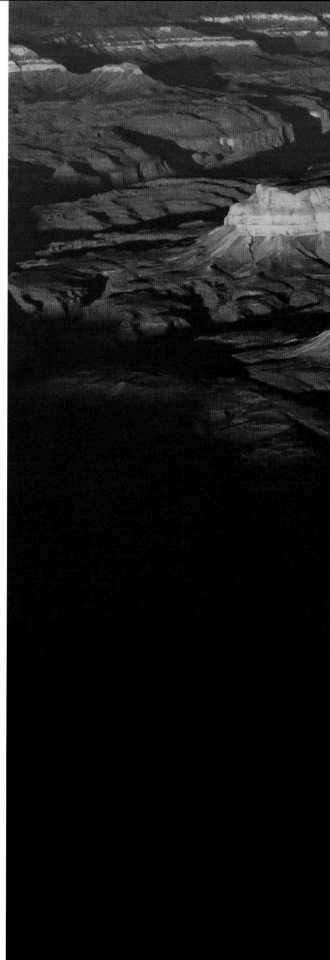

That night, as we soak up more silence under the current of stars flowing overhead, my canyon sense suggests it might be time to leave. Perhaps it is fatigue speaking after some 60 days of hiking more than 12 miles a day under a heavy pack. Or perhaps I'm more dehydrated than usual.

But as I focus my camera on yet another stunning vista that challenges my sense of scale, I'm certain of one thing. You never conquer this place. As the author Edward Abbey once mused, time, sweat, and blood in this place might begin to show something—maybe.

In the heat of spring, with summer knocking on the door, Kevin and I start hearing one message loud and clear—time to exit.

Soaking up the silence below the Dome just north of Mount Synella at the last light.

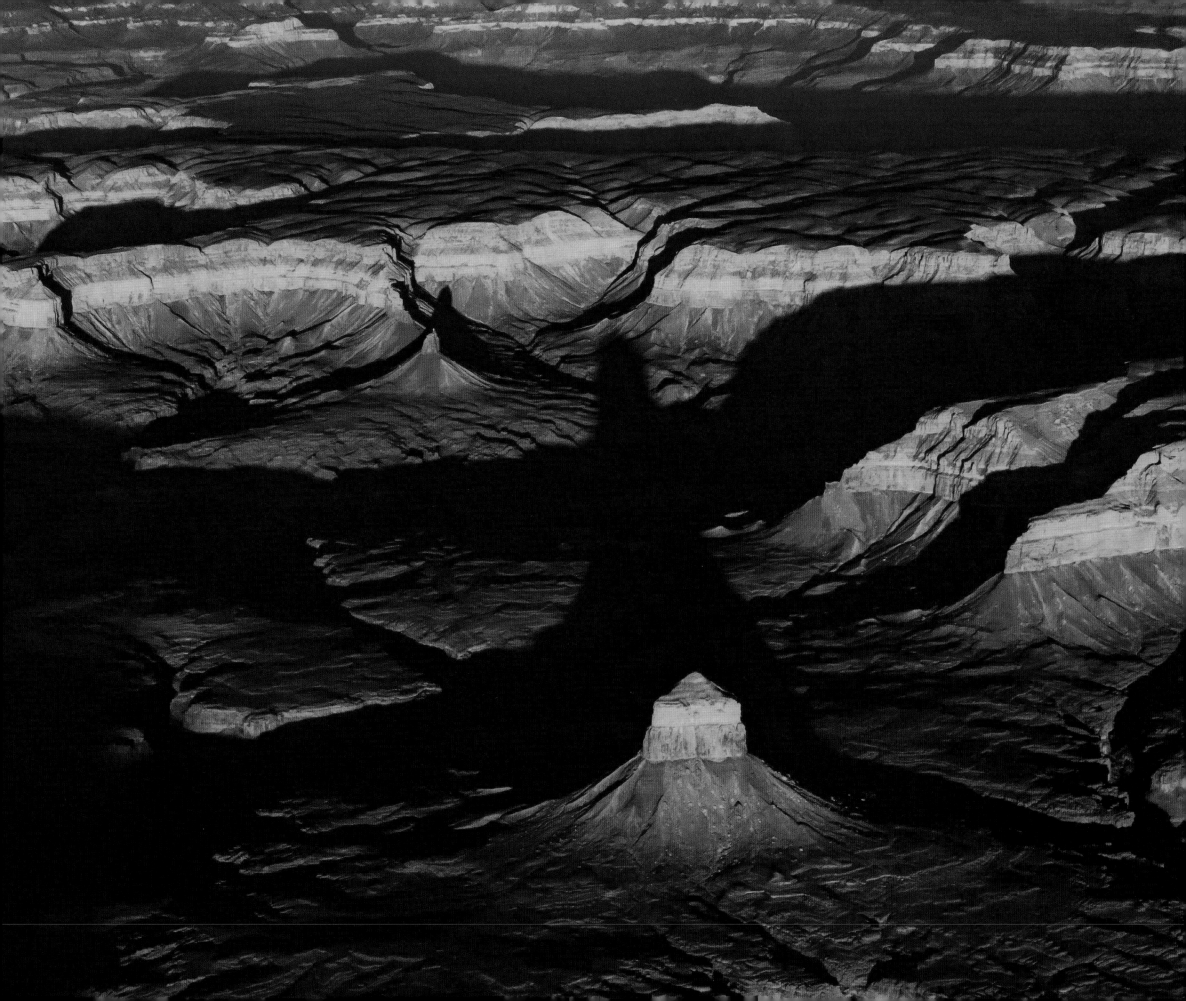

The ember-orange hues of dawn roll in near Parashant Canyon.

OVERLEAF
Finding water in the western Grand Canyon can force one to stretch their limits of thirst and flexibility (left). Spring temperatures quickly jump skyward, triggering cactus blooms to do the same (right).

PREVIOUS SPREAD
Gazing west across the fingers of the south rim reveals the erosion of the horizontal world into the verticality of the canyon (left). On remote, secret walls in the western Grand Canyon, time snaps backward like a rubber band when witnessing polychrome paintings dated 4,000 years or older (right).

The polished limestone inside Tuckup Canyon provides drinking water—and perspective.

OVERLEAF
A small seep creates a microhabitat of moss and lichen. There are approximately 64 species of moss and 195 lichen found in Grand Canyon National Park (left). Black brush and agave dot the butte known as "Mollie's Nipple" (right).

Dated at 350 million years old, the pink-hued
Temple Butte limestone layer is polished
smooth by years of flash floods.

OVERLEAF
Creative route finding is required when
negotiating up to the Sanup Plateau (left),
where spring erupts in swaths of color (right).

Moving downstream along the Tonto bench, wildlife is
secretive but present. There are approximately 41 reptiles
that live in the national park, 18 of which are lizards.

OVERLEAF
The Milky Way sweeps over the western realm of the park.
The distant glow of towns and cities is visible on the horizon.

SUMMER

QUARTERMASTER TO GRANDVIEW

The first rays of light illuminate a summer rain shower.

FOR SIMPLE RULES OF SAFETY, WE CHOOSE TO NOT HIKE DURING the heat of the summer. If we've learned one lesson, it is that the canyon respects no one, no matter how much time you've marveled, studied, and labored in its vastness.

Summer temperatures can easily push well above 110 degrees Fahrenheit, and when they do, the puzzles of water and rock start to lose connective pieces. In theory, one could simply hug the river and bushwhack all the way to the end of the park, but Kevin and I decide we want to explore the secrets of "the Godscape" beyond the banks of the Colorado. So we suspend our hiking mission and wait for the monsoonal rains of late summer to replenish the hidden springs and oases that sustain life, and for the desert temperatures to ease.

Although our hiking goal rests, my cameras don't. I have another photographic mission to "see" the canyon more fully—across its seasons and its layers. I want to understand and document what tourist traffic can look like when it goes relatively unchecked. As the mercury of the thermostat soars, I plunge back into the Big Ditch.

On the southwest corner of Grand Canyon National Park, where the Hualapai Reservation abuts the park's boundary, a new development has blossomed thanks to its proximity to the tourist market in nearby Las Vegas. In the early 2000s, the Hualapai tribe was granted permission by the Federal Aviation Administration to allow helicopters to fly and land below the rim of the canyon. Air tours have been allowed to fly within restricted flight corridors above the canyon for decades, but sightseeing helicopters were forbidden to duck below the rim inside the national park. When the air tours opened on Hualapai land, they created much-needed economic opportunity for the tribe. A number of Hualapai concluded that their time to prosper off the canyon's beauty had finally arrived. But few were able to anticipate what would actually happen.

Today, the three-mile corridor where helicopters are licensed to land—which is derisively referred to as "Heli Alley" by river runners— is one of the busiest helicopter landing areas in the world. And very few realize that the heliport within Hualapai lands on the river's edge directly abuts the border of the national park.

I'd witnessed this area once before when I floated through it on the final, dust-devil days of a raft trip. I was amazed when I saw and heard 16 helicopters in the air at once, flying up the canyon. For a moment, I wondered if I was witnessing an aerial display of sorts. But since I was floating downstream on a schedule, our flotilla kept moving and didn't linger. No one on the trip wanted to stop. "There's nothing to see here," one river guide said, sounding irritated by the blast of noise reminding him of the world we were about to reenter.

That trip, long ago, made me curious. What would it look and feel like to *walk* through this area? I also wanted to try and capture what traffic looked like over time. I had an idea.

So in mid-July, I recruit my friends Harlan Taney and Justin Clifton, two park lovers who reside in Flagstaff, Arizona, and know the canyon and the river well. With the temperature pegged at 118 degrees Fahrenheit at 4:00 p.m., we set out to experience "Heli Alley" via the river to document how many helicopter flights travel inside our most iconic national park in a day.

For eight hours on an average Tuesday, I do something I hadn't yet done on this entire journey. I sit in one place for an entire day. Cowering under a makeshift shade tarp, the three of us endure the furnace heat (115 degrees in the shade) and do nothing but count and document helicopters. By the end of the day, the drone and ringing of turbine engines reverberates in my ears.

It is an alarming contrast to the night. During the starlit hours, silence reigns beneath an orchestra of frogs lulling us to sleep. By sunrise, a different sound catapults us upright: the roar of tourists from Las Vegas checking off their bucket list, one helicopter flight at a time.

Weeks earlier, I sat at one of these landing zones. As a filmmaker and photographer who frequently uses helicopters, I wanted to take a sunrise flight to better understand this visitor experience. I'm acutely aware of the lure of such magical flying machines, so I wanted to experience how a mechanized tour compared to our time on foot.

The most glaring difference was that my Las Vegas Grand Canyon sunrise helicopter tour was fast. And expensive. In total, I spent 35 minutes in the canyon absorbing the views and scouting where we could hike—all while enjoying yogurt and champagne with roughly 40 other sightseers. Not once did the whine of a turbine engine cease. And before I realized it, I was back in Las Vegas for brunch, amazed by the flight and mystified by how little of the canyon awe I had experienced.

If someone had asked me what the Grand Canyon sounds like after that tour, I would not have been able to provide an answer. I never heard its desert song, or, more accurately, its silence. That void of sound inside the Grand Canyon is not defined by a profound emptiness, but rather the vibrant clarity of the sounds—mostly from wildlife and the river—that color it. One can't truly appreciate the song of birds, the baritone growl of rapids, the dull hum of bees, or the whoosh of bats feeding at sunrise until their ears are filled with the drowning silence beneath it.

Like all things, balance is important. And our sweltering foray into the world of industrial tourism showed me one thing. For eight hours a day, seven days a week, 365 days a year, "Heli Alley" blankets the great silence inside the Grand Canyon with noise, and yet few are aware of it.

I interviewed Hualapai tribal members after that trip and asked about their views on their newest tourism success. They told me the operation brought in $100 million annually, but one asked, "Where does that money go? We don't see it."

When I told them I'd counted 363 individual flights that day (according to records, some days see more than 400), one of their responses clearly outlined the dilemma in which the tribe has placed

A photographic merge illustrates a day of traffic in what is known as "Heli Alley." Each helicopter and boat represents one trip that crossed the camera's lens, totaling 363 helicopter flights in eight hours.

itself. "We need to make money, but the helicopters are a mess," he declared. "We are a hunting tribe. How can we hunt if we fill our lands with noise?"

A few weeks later, in August, I'm chasing after a different sound.

As an explosion of cumulus clouds converts the desert heat into angry black rain cells that prepare to unload their energy on the canyon, I return to the north rim. I'm hoping to document a monsoonal storm unleashing its might.

Once again, I join my friend Rich Rudow, and we set off for the remote overlooks of the canyon to chase weather. With a forecast for potential storm cells, we wait and watch above Kanab Creek. At first, I think we have been fooled by an unpredictable forecast. But Rich keeps staring at one dark cloud, saying, "Just wait."

By sunset, Rich is proven right. Our little cloud has expanded into a monster with pink plumes and black swirls billowing to the heavens.

"Are you ready for a light show?" Rich asks, as if talking to the canyon directly. He displays a boyish jubilation and anticipation.

As the last rays of light paint the clouds around us, a switch flips and the show begins. A flock of green parrots zooms past, cawing before diving into the canyon for safety. A warning, perhaps. Then the wind starts, at first with violent blasts from below and above, and then gray curtains of rain dance across our vista, trailed by a sweeping rainbow.

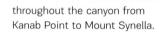

Monsoonal rain showers dance throughout the canyon from Kanab Point to Mount Synella.

Lightning bolts flare on the south rim, the thunder still too far away to be heard. Once again, the scale and distance of the landscape shatter my comprehension.

In silent disbelief, Rich and I attempt to predict where to aim our lenses next. And then, as the sun sets, the skies open around us.

Lightning flashes before us, behind us, and everywhere around us. The drums of thunder follow. It is as if a conductor of weather pointed to the percussion section of the storm orchestra and frantically waved his arms, signaling the bass drums to ignite.

As they echo and boom and echo again, Rich and I flee for cover. Flashes and spine-jarring cracks surround us. My hair starts to stand on end, and my skin tingles. I wonder if the next crack of thunder will be my last. But somehow, the storm turns and moves on. Then it circles us throughout the night. For the next 10 hours, flashes of lightning dance around the canyon as the Milky Way sweeps straight above us, perfectly visible through the eye of the storm.

We sleep little and awake to a final shower before the approaching dawn blushes pink and orange over Owl Eyes Bay. Dappled rays of light pierce the interior canyon. A tangerine glow reflects the results of the storm: in every direction, the once-dry potholes of the Esplanade ledge below are brimming with water everywhere.

It is time for Kevin and me to resume hiking again.

OVERLEAF
A late-afternoon storm cell unleashes lightning on the north rim.

The layered, shaded light of Mount
Synella and its neighboring rim spines
shimmer to the west (left) before the
sun colors the Great Thumb Mesa and
the north rim beyond (right).

The Milky Way glows above the canyon
as a summer storm recedes.

During the monsoon season, weather
around the canyon can abruptly
turn to billowing storms, sending
violent flash floods into inexpectant,
sun-soaked drainages miles away.

The flow of the Colorado River,
the lifeblood for 40 million people
in the Southwest, glides beneath
a moonlit wall below Deer Creek.

OVERLEAF
Rain showers soak the south rim (left),
sustaining life for many, such as a
tarantula hawk, one of the largest wasps
in the world, and a monarch butterfly
(right). The Grand Canyon is home to
292 species of butterflies and moths.

A spider tends its web (left) near the terminus of
Separation Canyon (right), a vast, fingered side canyon
near the western border of the park.

OVERLEAF
Sunrise cascades through the central corridor beneath a storm.

FINALE   DIAMOND CREEK TO GRAND WASH CLIFFS

In October, roughly 13 months after we took our first steps into the Grand Canyon, I descend off the rim into the great expanse below—carrying one camera, two lenses, a pack full of food, a day's worth of water, and a full ration of excitement and nerves. The thought of finishing this trek still feels like a distant, fuzzy idea. Finding the key to unlocking the maze of water scarcity never gets easier. Because we can only move with efficiency while carrying one day's worth of water (which is about six liters), we are never far from a looming thirst crisis, but I'm excited to document some of the last and least-visited secrets of the park.

We have roughly 100 miles to hike before we cross the Grand Wash Cliffs, where the physical Grand Canyon melts into the Mojave Desert. The official national park boundary is about 15 miles earlier, but you can't exit the "high church of the canyon," as so many river runners call it, unless you pass through that final gateway.

To celebrate our final miles, Kevin and I agree that sharing the tail end of our journey with Rich Rudow, the man who started with us and taught us so much along the way, makes perfect sense. Kelly McGrath and Mathieu Brown also agree to join us for sections. They are the backbone of a community that has supported us throughout this journey. And few care more about this landscape than these three—so it's fitting we all march to the end together.

For the first two days, we scramble through the secret subway systems north of Diamond Creek. With each hidden slot we descend, we sweat and zigzag our way back up to the Tonto and Esplanade benches to explore more.

Ascending an Ancestral Puebloan route that is estimated to be more than 900 years old through a break in the Redwall layer.

At the end of a 12-hour hiking push, we are once again reminded of the danger of the place. A spring that Rich had depended on once before (and from which we planned to draw water) proves to be bone dry. We resort to licking dusty thimbles of rainwater from tiny rock depressions. That night, we bed down with empty water bottles and parched throats on a heap of polished rocks.

The following day, we discover the spring has relocated two miles down the side canyon—further evidence of the canyon's dynamic, ever-changing landscape.

On another afternoon, we climb five hours and some 3,500 vertical feet up a tributary canyon following pictographs and polychrome paintings until, at the very top, we encounter a nearly petrified cedar log whose notched steps confirm we are on an ancient trail. Rich believes the route to be at least 900 years old and once served as an Ancestral Puebloan trade path. Clearly, we are not the first to visit this remote side canyon.

As we move up and down through the final reaches of the canyon, I begin to realize that the gems and majesty of this rocky cathedral are not limited to the more popular pockets that lie far to the east. Out here during our final days in the canyon, we discover more ancient art, more bighorn sheep, more potsherds, and more rattlesnakes, coyotes, mule deer, bobcats, quail, frogs, tarantulas, and tarantula hawks—more in our final days than we did in the previous 600 miles of our journey.

One evening at dusk, just as the sun kisses the buttes goodnight, a cacophony of bird noise explodes in a flowering tree near the black brush where we are nestled. The eruption is deafening. A joyous

collection of mating calls and chatter. Songbird happy hour. Maybe we've finally started hearing the landscape.

One thing is for sure, because one sound, above all the rest, gets louder with every mile. The closer we get to the end, the more we hear the ubiquitous drone of helicopters during daylight hours. Surprisingly, it permeates every tributary and ledge and layer of rock we navigate.

On our seventh day, under the glimmer of starlight, we reach the Colorado River and collapse. Seven hours later, before the sun has touched the inner canyon walls, we hear the first turbines.

Once again, we are back inside "Heli Alley." By 8:00 a.m., even before we have finished our coffee, we count 25 flights.

Over the course of the next 10 hours, we walk downstream directly across from roughly a dozen separate landing pads. The air tours come in waves and, at times, swarms. A few of the choppers zoom just 50 feet over our heads, blasting us in rotor wash. It is illegal

A storm of silt and dust blows through Quartermaster (opposite), where air-tour operators are approved to land helicopters near the park boundary on Hualapai land (above).

to fly over the park, but many do so, claiming safety reasons later. Throughout the day, I count helicopters again and end up tallying more than 300 individual flights.

At sunset, the deep silence returns. And then, somewhere in the distance, frogs start to croak.

Three days later, on a Sunday afternoon in early November, we find ourselves staring at three rusty metal posts roughly five feet apart, pounded into the dirt. The northwestern corner of Grand Canyon National Park is so remote that this is the only marker delineating its boundary.

Kevin and I stare at the end of our yearlong goal—and we then stride through the poles and exit Grand Canyon National Park. As we step across, we exchange high fives. Just for fun, I do a quick tally of some key stats from our journey: 750-plus miles, 71 days, eight pairs of shoes,

We take a final, jubilant step across the national park's northwestern border (above) before hiking out of Pearce Canyon and exiting the Grand Wash Cliffs (opposite).

four sprained ankles, one broken finger, one case of hyponatremia, hundreds of cactus needles . . . the list goes on.

We share a celebratory howl, and then keep hiking. While it's true that we've left the park, the geographical exit of the canyon still lies ahead—16 miles to the west and some 3,000 vertical feet below us.

As we scramble into a setting sun on sore knees, we add up the more important metrics of the walk—namely, what lessons the canyon taught us. Even though its rock and geography appear unmovable, untouched by our human footprint, the canyon has revealed a fragility that is defined not by geologic time, but by the magic of the many connected ecosystems thriving inside. And all of it—the dirt and dust and rock and cactus and colossal record of time—is overlaid by a river of starlight and a liquid silence more profound than words can express or images can capture.

The silence of this natural wonder starkly contrasts with the noise we make everywhere else, even as the canyon invites us to carry some of that silence within ourselves as we return to the world beyond the rims. As I wonder if any of my images have captured that, I find myself pondering an even deeper question: Is it possible that this journey by foot, along with the photographic record that it has yielded, might help illuminate and underscore what we all share—as well as what we all risk losing—if we fail to protect this vast abyss by foregoing the urge to transform its beauty into cash and simply leaving it as it is?

While the answer to that question is for others to decide, I do know one thing. After spending so many months drenched in the silence and magic of the seventh natural wonder of the world, I know there is only one place that looks and sounds like this.

A double rainbow briefly hovers
above the rim.

OVERLEAF
Sunset washes across the Sanup
Plateau below Burnt Canyon Point.

Although rarely visited, the labyrinth of tributary drainages in the western Grand Canyon are as complex, archaeologically rich, and massive as any in the entire national park.

Rock steps and cedar ladders are evidence of Ancestral Puebloan routes and reminders that many traveled by foot through these side canyons centuries before.

OVERLEAF
Slot canyons such as Climax are as deep and convoluted as any in all of the Grand Canyon.

The fleeting, colorful bloom of a datura is one among an
estimated 650 wildflower species that grow in the canyon.

OVERLEAF
A final salute to the silence-soaked seventh natural
wonder of the world, a geologic time machine that
instills wonder and humility like no other.

ACKNOWLEDGMENTS

THIS COLLECTION OF PHOTOGRAPHY AND WORDS, WHICH AROSE from a line of footprints between the Colorado River and the rim of the Grand Canyon, would not exist without the support of a remarkable community of canyon lovers, colleagues, friends, and family who not only enriched the journey but also enabled it. Photographing the seventh natural wonder of the world, perhaps the most documented landscape on earth, with a fresh look from its remote ribs, its colored contours, and its vast, humbling space, took an army of gracious, helping hands and experienced experts.

First and foremost, the Grand Canyon National Park staff and especially the backcountry office were instrumental in making this book a reality. Thanks to former park superintendent Dave Uberuaga for the support, Betsy Donehoo for the permits, Pamela Edwards for the initial inspiration, Todd Seliga for the western support (and salad), and all the staff who devote so much time to a place they love. Best of luck to Chris Lehnertz managing this crown jewel of perspective.

To Theresa McMullan, Susan Schroeder, and the team at the Grand Canyon Association, a profound thanks for the enthusiastic support and partnership.

Without the support of the National Geographic Society and Magazine, this long walk would not have endured its many challenges. Susan Goldberg, thanks for giving this journey a wider voice. Sadie Quarrier, your dedication as a photo editor and friend is only rivaled by the size of the canyon.

My hat goes off to Kayla Lindquist with Sony for directing me to the one camera and one lens that would document this marathon.

The maze of rock, water, and time is seen above Kanab Creek and Mount Synella.

Mike St. Pierre and Hyperlite Mountain Gear, kudos for lightening our load. My family is grateful to Delorme for helping us stay in touch via its satellite systems, all powered by the sun thanks to Goal Zero.

Understanding the issues that surround Grand Canyon National Park and the 11 Native American tribal lands is as complex as the geology within the canyon. Navigating these issues requires a network of people with insight and experience. I am grateful to Roger Clark and Ethan Aumack of the Grand Canyon Trust, Renae Yellowhorse, Jason Nez, Sarana Riggs, Rita Bilogody, Da Wa, Deon Ben, and all the devoted families behind Save the Confluence.

Grasping the maze of fresh water that flows through the canyon is paramount when you depend on it daily. Thanks to Larry Stevens, the Carletta Tilousi family, and the members of the Havasupai tribe for consistently reminding the world about the importance of this often overlooked issue. I'm grateful to Bennett Wakayuta and his community within the Hualapai tribe for their perspective on the western Grand Canyon and finding balance between beauty and economic viability. Merv Yoyetewa, thanks for living the motto, "Don't worry, be Hopi."

Huge gratitude to Harlan Taney and Four Corner Film Logistics for coordinating our connection to civilization and much more. Blake McCord, Justin Clifton, Chad de Alva, Steve Hatch, Scott Perry, OARS Rafting, Brad Dimock, Gavin Heaton, and the Bar 10 Ranch all carried loads of hospitality on this front, which were greatly appreciated. John Dillon, your aerial perspective went above and beyond—thanks for the wings. Jeanne-Philippe (J. P.) Clark, we'd have lost even more weight without your food cache support. Thanks for pulling us out at South Canyon. Doctors John Tveten and Tom Myers, my cactus tattoos and salt balance thank you personally.

Hampton Sides, your literary magic is cherished. Thanks for gracing these images.

Michelle Smith, I'm grateful for your endless patience, which served as a rudder throughout this entire project, and Jeremy Joseph, thanks for making these images sing.

A special thanks goes to the team at Rizzoli for your partnership on this adventure, especially Jim Muschett, Susi Oberhelman, Candice Fehrman, and Jessica Napp.

Last but not least, there is a group of dust-encrusted canyon lovers who showed us how to follow the lion tracks, sheep trails, and ancient routes through the Redwall breaks. Your expertise helped us find our feet inside that magical maze of rock and time. Mathieu Brown and Kelly McGrath, your energy is contagious. I wish I could bottle it.

Amy Martin, your eye for imagery and archaeology is inspiring. Chris Atwood and Dave Nally, thanks for all the assists and electrolytes. Andrew Holycross, Chris Forsyth, and everyone in the greater Grand Canyon hiking community—I'm grateful you taught me the difference between "what you want and what you need."

Rich Rudow, the leader of this hiking herd, thanks for making this project come to life and sticking with it to the end. I still owe you some soy sauce packs. To many more photo missions and "Rutrow" moments.

To Kevin Fedarko, my compadre in this venture, thanks for teaching me how to see this world in a new way, beyond the limits of imagery. And most importantly, thanks for deciding that 750-plus miles on foot, the journey of our lives, was a good idea.

Thank You | Ahéhee | Kwakwha | Han kya | Han kyo | Elahkwa
(English | Navajo | Hopi | Hualapai | Havasupai | Zuni)

Agave stalks shoot skyward below the north rim (opposite). Windows of sunlight highlight layers of deep time on the south rim (above).

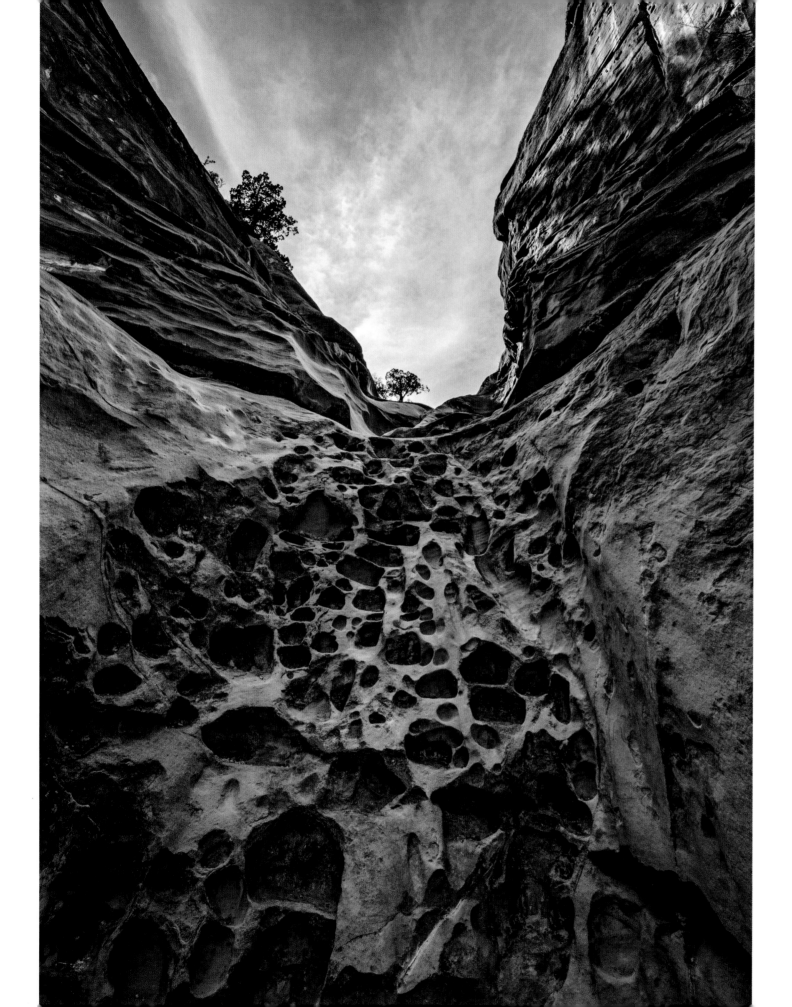

First published in the United States of America
in 2018
Rizzoli International Publications, Inc.
300 Park Avenue South
New York, NY 10010
www.rizzoliusa.com

Photographs and Text © 2018 Pete McBride
Foreword by Hampton Sides
Introduction by Kevin Fedarko

Associate Publisher: James Muschett
Project Editor: Candice Fehrman
Book Design: Susi Oberhelman
Endpaper Map: Jeremy Collins

Grand
Canyon
Association

The Grand Canyon Association is the official nonprofit
partner of Grand Canyon National Park. For more
information, please visit www.grandcanyon.org.

2018 2019 2020 2021 / 10 9 8 7 6 5 4 3 2 1

Printed in China

ISBN-13: 978-0-8478-6304-4

Library of Congress Catalog Control Number:
2018935588

LEFT: A naturally sculpted rock ladder leads
to water somewhere in the West.
PAGES 2–3: Sunrise washes over Kelly Point
and the western Grand Canyon.
PAGES 4–5: Layers of light stack among the
buttes and temples in the canyon as the
San Francisco Peaks loom to the south.
PAGES 6–7: A full moon rises over the
canyon's chief architect, the Colorado River,
as the Nankoweap Granaries—roughly
900-year-old Ancestral Puebloan storage
caves—glow by headlamp.